Experiments with Motion

3-99

Getting Started in Science

Experiments with

Motion

Robert Gardner

ENSLOW PUBLISHERS, INC.

44 Fadem Road	P.O. Box 38
Box 699	Aldershot
Springfield, N.J. 07081	Hants GU12 6BP
U.S.A.	U.K.

Library of Congress Cataloging-in-Publication Data

Gardner, Robert, 1929–
    Experiments with motion / Robert Gardner.
        p. cm. — (Getting started in science)
    Includes bibliographical references and index.
    ISBN 0-89490-667-4
    1. Motion—Experiments—Juvenile literature. [1. Motion—
Experiments. 2. Experiments.] I. Title. II. Series: Gardner,
Robert, 1929– Getting started in science.
QC133.5.G37 1995
531'.112'078—dc20

                                  95-8543
                                      CIP
                                        AC

Printed in the United States of America

10 9 8 7 6 5 4 3 2

Illustration Credits: Kimberly Austin Daly

Cover photo: Enslow Publishers, Inc.

Contents

Introduction   4

1 Motion Inside a Coasting
     Spaceship   7

2 How Animals Move 33

3 Vehicles That Stop and Go 58

4 Things That Go Bump in the Night
     (or Day) 85

Answers to Puzzlers and Surprises . . 104

Further Reading 110

Index 111

Introduction

Playing with toys and other things that move and bump into each other is fun. It is also a good way to get started in science. Toys provide a pathway to science because they can serve as the bases for many experiments—experiments that involve how things move, how they stop, how they change direction, how they collide, and other science-related ideas.

Experiments with Motion will allow you to carry out investigations using simple everyday objects and materials more often associated with play than with science. Bicycles, toy trucks and cars, wagons, marbles, modeling clay, paper airplanes, and balloons will all be used in the experiments found in this book. These experiments will lead you to a number of scientific discoveries, principles, puzzlers, surprises, and measuring techniques. At the same time, you will become aware of how science works, because you will be investigating the world as scientists do.

Some experiments will be preceded by an explanation of a scientific principle. In some cases, the explanation will involve doing additional experiments in order to help you better understand the principle. Once you understand the basic idea, you should have enough information to allow you to answer questions and interpret results in the experiments that come after the principle. Some of these experiments might start you on a path leading to a science fair project.

A few puzzlers and surprises related to the experiments are scattered throughout the book. The answers to these puzzlers and surprises can be found by doing more experiments or by turning to the back of the book. But don't turn to the answers right away. See if you can come up with your own solutions to the problems or questions first. Then compare your answers with the ones given.

The experiments and activities included in this book were chosen because they are related to making things move or stop moving. Most of them are safe and can be investigated without expensive equipment. If an experiment requires the use of a knife, a flame, or anything that has a potential for danger, you will be asked to work with an adult. Please do so! The purpose of such a request is to protect you from getting hurt.

)

Sir Isaac Newton was probably the greatest scientist and mathematician who ever lived, but Newton did not think there was any limit to speed. It was Albert Einstein who showed us that nature does have a speed limit. It is the speed of light—300,000 kilometers per second (186,000 miles per second)!

Motion Inside a Coasting Spaceship

Sir Isaac Newton (1642–1727) was the first person to really understand motion. His success was due to his ability to think about what motion would be like without friction and without gravity.

Most of the motions we find on earth involve *friction*. Friction occurs when two surfaces rub against one another. If you roll a ball slowly across the floor, the ball's speed decreases and eventually it stops. It stops because the friction between the ball and the floor pushes against the ball and reduces its motion. The same thing happens when you slide into a base while playing baseball. If you did not slide, you would overrun the base. By sliding, friction between your body and the earth pushes against you. This force of friction pushing against your body reduces your speed and finally brings you to rest before you move past the base.

Gravity is the force that pulls you toward the earth. No matter how high or how hard you jump, you fall back to the ground because the earth pulls on you. This pull is called gravity. The earth's gravitational pull does not just affect you. It pulls on everyone and everything. It pulls on the moon, the sun, and the other planets as well. But the moon, sun, and planets pull on the earth, too. They also pull on you, and you on them. Because you are much closer to the earth than you are to the sun or the moon, the earth's pull on you is much stronger than the pull the others have on you. As a result, you remain "fastened" quite securely to the earth.

Newton said his ideas about motion were "built on the shoulders of giants." One of those giants was Galileo Galilei (1564–1642). Galileo realized that without friction, a moving object would continue to move forever. He built a smooth, wooden trough (like the gutter in a modern bowling alley) with inclines at both ends, like the one shown in Figure 1a. When he let a ball roll down the left incline, he found that it would rise to almost the same height on the right incline. If he made the incline at the right end of the trough longer and less steep (see Figure 1b), the ball would still rise to nearly the same height as before. Galileo was aware that if the right incline was eliminated, the ball would roll forever if there were no friction to slow its motion.

Galileo's idea led Newton to his first law of motion. To understand Newton's laws of motion, we will imagine that we are on a spaceship. Our spaceship is so far away from all stars, moons, and planets that there is no gravity pulling on the ship or anything in it. It is drifting along at a steady speed towards a distant galaxy.

You are holding a ball in this spaceship. You open your fingers and release the ball. The ball remains where it was; it does not move! There is no gravity to make it fall, and you did not push it in any direction. You have discovered part II of Newton's first law of motion—a basic principle of science often known as the law of inertia.

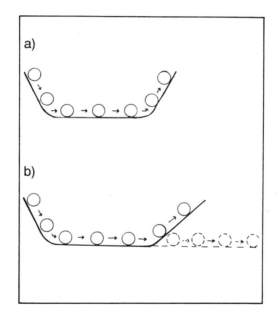

1) Galileo knew that a ball released on the left ramp would rise to very nearly the same height on the right ramp. If there were no friction, it would rise to exactly the same height. When the right ramp was made longer and less steep, the ball rolled farther. Without the right ramp and without friction, Galileo realized the ball would roll forever.

Science Principle: The First Law of Motion, Part II

If an object is at rest, it will remain at rest unless a push or a pull (a force) is applied to it.

1.1 OBJECTS AT REST TEND TO REMAIN AT REST

To do this experiment you will need:
- plastic cup
- small sheet of plastic
- water
- table

You can see that Newton was right about objects at rest. It is obvious that things do not move unless someone or something exerts a force (a push or a pull) on them. What is not as obvious is that the force must act for some time to produce any motion. To see that this is so, half-fill a plastic cup with water. Place the cup of water near the far end of a small sheet of smooth plastic near the edge of a table, as shown in Figure 2. Pull the near end of the plastic sheet with a quick, horizontal tug. You will find that the cup of water remains in place. What happens if you pull the plastic sheet slowly?

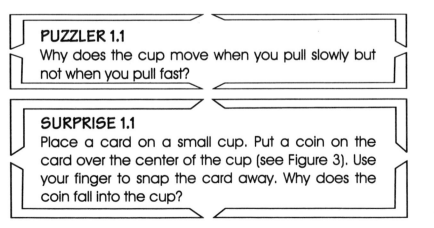

PUZZLER 1.1
Why does the cup move when you pull slowly but not when you pull fast?

SURPRISE 1.1
Place a card on a small cup. Put a coin on the card over the center of the cup (see Figure 3). Use your finger to snap the card away. Why does the coin fall into the cup?

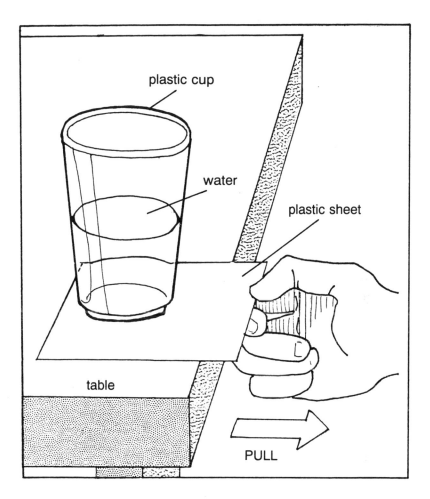

plastic cup

water

plastic sheet

table

PULL

2) The magician's tablecloth trick is an example of Newton's first law of motion, part II.

Science Principle: The First Law of Motion, Part I

An object in motion will continue to move in a straight line at a constant speed unless a force acts on it.

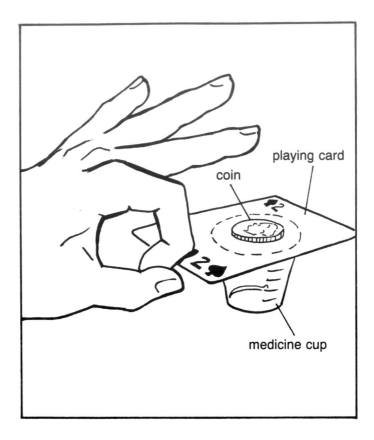

playing card

coin

medicine cup

3) The coin-in-the-cup experiment is done by snapping the card away with your finger.

1.2 THE FIRST LAW OF MOTION, PART I

Let us return to our spaceship. There, we find the ball exactly where you released it. You give the ball a gentle push and it moves away from you along a straight-line path at what seems to be a steady speed, as shown in Figure 4. To see if it really is moving at a steady speed, an astronaut makes some measurements. She notes the ball's position after one-second intervals and records the data and speed in a table. Her results are shown in Table 1.

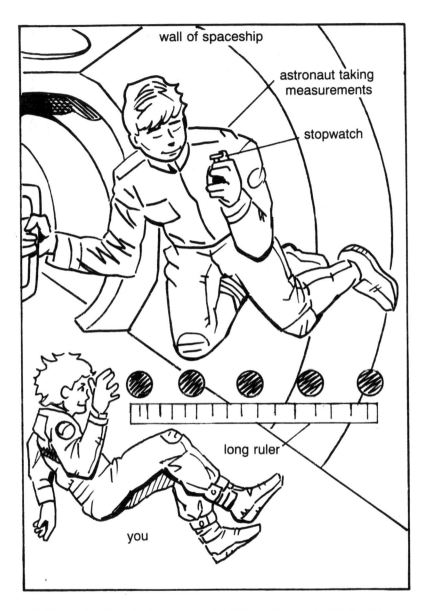

4) You give the ball a push. Another astronaut measures
the ball's position at one-second intervals.

TABLE 1:

THE POSITION AND SPEED OF THE BALL IN THE SPACESHIP AT ONE-SECOND INTERVALS AFTER IT WAS GIVEN A SLIGHT PUSH.

Time (seconds)	Position (meters)	(feet)	Speed (kph)	(mph)
0.0	0.0	0.0	0.0	1.0
1.0	0.46	1.5	1.61	1.0
2.0	0.92	3.0	1.61	1.0
3.0	1.38	4.5	1.61	1.0
4.0	1.84	6.0	1.61	1.0

As the results of the experiment show, after the ball is given a small push, it moves along a straight line at a steady (constant) speed. You have observed part I of Newton's first law of motion.

Parts I and II together make up Newton's first law of motion. You probably realize that part II is really a special case of part I. In part II, the speed happens to be zero. Therefore, the body keeps that zero speed until a force makes it move.

1.3   MOTION WHEN NO FORCE ACTS

To do this experiment you will need:
- adult to help you
- small sharp nail
- wooden spool
- round balloon
- air-hockey table
- puck or sharp knife
- sheet of cardboard
- glue or tape
- sharp pencil
- twistie
- smooth surface such as the top of a kitchen counter

You have seen that an object does not move unless a force is applied to it. The first law of motion, part I, says that if an object is moving, it will continue to move in the same direction with the same speed unless a force acts on it. We seldom see an object on Earth coasting at a constant speed. This is because friction is present in the motions we experience. Our shoes rub against the floor, automobile tires rub against the road, train wheels rub against steel tracks, and even airplanes rub against the air. You can come close to observing frictionless motion—the kind Newton imagined—by watching a puck slide across the surface of a level air-hockey table. Give the puck a slight push and watch it continue to move. What do you notice about its speed? What do you notice about its direction of motion? Do your observations agree with the first law of motion?

Building an Air Car

If you do not have an air-hockey table, you can build a "frictionless" air car from a piece of cardboard, a spool, and a balloon, as shown in Figure 5. **Ask an adult** to use a sharp knife to cut out a square piece of cardboard about 10 to 12 centimeters (4 to 5 inches) on a side. Push a small, sharp nail through the center of the smooth, bottom side of the square and then remove the nail. Glue or tape an empty wooden spool onto the top of the square; the hole through the spool should be over the hole in the cardboard square. If the hole through the spool's axis is covered with paper, push a sharp pencil through the paper. You should be able to see through the long axis of the spool.

After the glue has dried, blow up a round balloon. Tie off the neck of the balloon with a twistie and attach it to the spool. Place the air car on a smooth surface such as the top of a kitchen counter and remove the twistie. Give the air car a gentle push. It should slide along the counter at nearly constant speed. If it does not slide smoothly, use

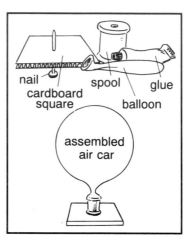

nail   spool   glue
cardboard
square   balloon

assembled
air car

5) You can make a nearly frictionless air car from cardboard, a spool, glue, and a balloon.

SURPRISE 1.2

Place a hard-boiled egg and an uncooked egg on a counter or table top. Spin the hard-boiled egg. While it is spinning, stop it for a moment. Then release it. You will find that the egg remains at rest. Repeat the experiment with the uncooked egg. This time, the egg starts moving again when you release it. Can you explain why? Compare your answer with the one given on page 104.

a sharp pencil to widen the hole in the bottom of the card-board or **ask an adult** to trim any roughness along the edges of the cardboard with a sharp knife. Then try it again.

1.4   THE SECOND LAW OF MOTION

Let us return once more to our distant spaceship. You stop the ball that was moving slowly inside the spaceship. Then, you release it so that it is at rest again. To see what hap-pens when you apply a steady (constant) force to an object, you attach a rubber band to the ball. To keep the force on the ball constant, you stretch the rubber band the same amount all the time you pull on it, as shown in Figure 6. You notice that the ball begins to move and that it keeps moving faster and faster. An astronaut records its speed every second using automatic timers connected to a speedometer. His record of the ball's speed while the constant force acts on it is shown in Table 2. As you can see, the ball's speed increases by 3.2 kilometers (2 miles) per hour for every second you pull on it.

TABLE 2:
THE BALL'S SPEED AT ONE-SECOND INTERVALS WHEN A CONSTANT PULL (FORCE) ACTS ON IT.

Time	Speed	
(seconds)	(kph)	(mph)
0	0.0	0.0
1	3.2	2.0
2	6.4	4.0
3	9.6	6.0
4	12.8	8.0

6) A ball's speed is measured every second while a constant force acts on it.

When an object's speed increases, we say it is *accelerating*. If its speed increases uniformly (by the same amount each second), we say that it has a *constant acceleration*. Is the acceleration shown in Table 2 constant? By how much does the speed increase every second?

Next, you stretch the rubber band so that you pull twice as hard on the ball. Again, someone measures the ball's speed and finds that it increases uniformly with time, as shown in Table 3.

TABLE 3:
THE BALL'S SPEED AT ONE-SECOND INTERVALS WHEN A FORCE THAT IS TWICE AS BIG ACTS ON IT.

| Time | Speed | |
(seconds)	(kph)	(mph)
0	0.0	0.0
1	6.4	4.0
2	12.8	8.0
3	19.3	12.0
4	25.6	16.0

By how much did the speed increase every second when the force was doubled? What happens to the acceleration when you double the force acting on the ball? (Hint: Compare the data in Tables 2 and 3 to see by how much the speed increases every second.)

You repeat the experiment once more. You stretch the rubber band by the same amount that you did in the experiment that gave the data in Table 2. But this time, you attach a second identical ball to the first one so that you are pulling twice as much matter. (Newton would have said that you doubled the *mass*. He defined the amount of matter in an object as its mass.) Your partner records the speed of the ball with twice as much mass at one-second intervals and records the data shown in Table 4.

TABLE 4:

THE SPEED OF TWICE AS MUCH MASS AT ONE-SECOND INTERVALS WHEN A CONSTANT PULL (FORCE) ACTS ON IT.

Time (seconds)	Speed	
	(kph)	(mph)
0	0.0	0.0
1	1.6	1.0
2	3.2	2.0
3	4.8	3.0
4	6.4	4.0

By how much does the speed increase every second? What happens to the acceleration when the same force is applied to twice as much mass? (Hint: Compare the data in Tables 2 and 4 to see by how much the speed increases every second.)

PUZZLER 1.2
What can you conclude from these three spaceship experiments and all the data you have
collected in Tables 2, 3, and 4? The information
you have collected in these three experiments is
the basis for Newton's second law of motion.

Science Principle: Newton's Second Law of Motion

When a constant force acts on an object, the object accelerates uniformly in the direction of the force. The acceleration is proportional to the force. (This means that when the force is doubled, the acceleration doubles.) The acceleration is inversely proportional to the mass. (This means that when the mass is doubled, the acceleration is half as much.)

1.5   MOTION WHEN A CONSTANT FORCE ACTS

To do this experiment you will need:
- long, thin rubber band
- small heavy objects (books, stones, or sand will work well)
- scissors
- large toy car or truck

Find a long, thin rubber band. Use scissors to cut the rubber band. Attach one end of the rubber band to a fairly heavy toy truck or car, and place it on a smooth level surface, as shown in Figure 7a. Hold the truck with one hand while you stretch the rubber band a small amount with the other hand. Release the truck and try to keep the rubber band stretched by the same amount as you pull the truck forward. Does the truck accelerate?

Repeat the experiment. But this time, stretch the rubber band more than you did before. Again, release the truck and try to keep the rubber band stretched by the same larger amount as you pull the truck forward. How

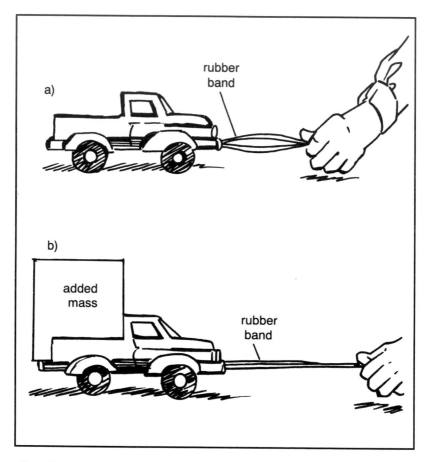

7a) A constant force is applied to a toy truck with a rubber band. A bigger force can be applied by stretching the rubber band more.

b) What happens to the acceleration if mass is added to the truck and the force stays the same?

does the increased force affect the truck's acceleration?

Next, add mass to the truck (see Figure 7b). You might pile books, stones, sand, or some other small heavy objects onto the truck. Repeat the experiment with the rubber band stretched about the same amount as in the last experiment. What effect does the bigger mass have on the truck's acceleration?

1.6   THE THIRD LAW OF MOTION

Let us return once more to our spaceship. There you join a fellow astronaut to carry out a simple experiment. The two of you work your way to the center of a large room in the spaceship where you are both at rest. (Of course, both you and the ship are moving through space at constant speed. We use the words "at rest" to mean the same thing that they do on earth, which is also moving through space at a very high speed.)

Testing the Third Law of Motion

Your astronaut friend gives you a gentle push with her hand, as shown in Figure 8. During the time she pushes on you, you accelerate away from her. Once the two of you are no longer in contact, you move away from your friend at a constant speed until you collide with the wall of the ship. Your astronaut friend has the same experience. She accelerates in the other direction (away from you) during the time she pushes on you. She then moves away from you at a constant speed.

A rope is stretched across the room. Once you and your partner come to rest by grabbing handles at opposite ends of the room, you hold one end of the rope while your fellow astronaut holds the other end. You both release the handles and you give the rope a gentle tug, pulling your partner toward you. While you are pulling, she accelerates toward you. Once the tug is over, she continues to move toward you, but at constant

8) A gentle push causes both astronauts to accelerate and then move at steady speeds in opposite directions.

speed. Using the rope you pulled on her, but she must have pulled on you as well because you find that you are accelerating toward her. Once the tug is over, you continue to move toward her at a steady speed. You both move in opposite directions toward one another until you meet near the center of the room.

Are the actions in these experiments examples of a universal law of motion, or are they limited to living things? To find out, you watch as two astronauts in the spaceship take two metal blocks, place a small spring between them, and squeeze them together. They tie a string around the blocks and spring, as shown in Figure 9. With the blocks at rest, one of them burns the string. The spring allows the blocks to push against

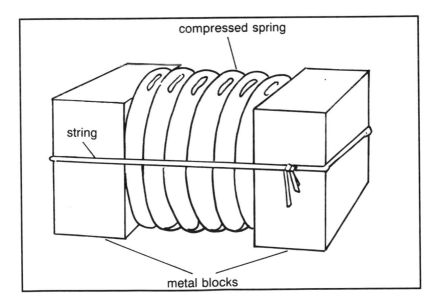

compressed spring

string

metal blocks

9) What will happen when the string is burned?

one another, and they move apart just as you and your fellow astronaut did. You conclude, as Newton did, that these motions apply to everything. They are examples of a universal law of motion—Newton's third law of motion.

Science Principle: Newton's Third Law of Motion

If one object exerts a force on a second object, the second object exerts an equal force in the opposite direction on the first one.

This law is often stated another way: For every action, there is an equal and opposite reaction. As you sit reading this book, you push downward on the chair in which you are sitting. The chair, in turn, pushes upward on you. When you stand up, you push on the floor with all your weight and the floor pushes upward on you with an equal force, so that you neither rise to the ceiling nor fall through the floor. When you walk, you push backward against the ground with your foot. The ground (the earth) exerts an equal force forward on your foot. We see you move forward because of the earth's force on you. But we do not see the earth move. Its mass is so large that its motion in the opposite direction is too small to be noticed.

1.7 EXPERIENCE AND OBSERVE THE THIRD LAW OF MOTION

To do this experiment you will need:

- friend to help you
- medicine ball
- oblong balloon
- water
- rubber stopper
- Styrofoam cup
- flexible plastic drinking straws
- rubber bands
- ice skates, roller skates (or blades), or skateboards
- rope
- high-pressure water gun
- large sink or bathtub
- measuring cup
- pencil
- scissors
- thread
- string
- level ice or smooth, level ground
- seltzer tablets

Experiencing the Third Law

The best way to understand the third law of motion is to experience it. This is easy to do. All you have to do is push against a wall. Can you feel the wall push back against you? You experience the third law every time you push on something. Pushing against a wall, however, is not very satisfying because nothing moves. You do not usually move away from the object you push on because friction keeps your feet firmly planted on the ground. By pushing against a wall, which is attached to the earth, your hands, in effect, are pushing against your feet.

If you have ice skates, roller skates, or a skateboard—something that dramatically reduces the friction between your feet and the earth—you can experience motion in response to the third law. Stand behind a friend who is also on skates or a skateboard.

While you are both at rest on ice or on a smooth, level surface, tell your friend that you are going to push him or her. Then give your friend a moderate push. Which way does your friend move? Which way do you move? When you pushed on your friend, how do you know that he or she also pushed back on you?

If possible, repeat the experiment with someone who is much bigger and someone who is much smaller than you. Who moves faster after the push—the bigger or the smaller person? While still on skates or a skateboard, hold one end of a 3-meter (10-foot) rope. Have your friend, also on skates or a skateboard, hold the other end. Pull on your friend using the tightly stretched rope. What was the direction of the force on your friend? What was the direction of the force on you? Which way did you move? Which way did your friend move?

If you can make friction very small, you can experience the third law in other ways. Hold a heavy ball, such as a medicine ball, while standing on ice skates, roller skates, or a skateboard. Using both hands, push the ball away from your chest with as much force as possible. Which way do you move when the ball moves away from you? If the friction is very small, you may even experience the third law by shooting a high-pressure water gun while standing on skates or a skateboard. Which way do you move when you shoot the water? Which way does the water move?

Observing the Third Law of Motion

There are many ways to observe the third law of motion. Here are a few.

1. Blow up an oblong balloon and release it. What evidence do you have of the third law of motion? What does the balloon push out through its open end? What pushes back against the balloon?

2. The balloon does not have to push air; it can push water as well. Fill a large sink or bathtub with water. Attach an oblong balloon to a faucet and fill it with water. Seal the balloon's neck with your fingers, remove it from the faucet, and place it in the water-filled sink or tub. Release the balloon. What makes the balloon "submarine" move through the water? What evidence do you have of the third law of motion?

To see what is happening more clearly, repeat the experiment. But this time, put several drops of food coloring inside the balloon before you attach It to the faucet. What do you see after you place the water-filled balloon in the sink or tub?

3. Suspend a plastic bottle or tube from strings, as shown in Figure 10a. Be sure the mouth of the bottle or tube does not face a window or anything that might be broken. Break one or two seltzer tablets in half. Tip the bottle or tube and pour in a small amount of water (see Figure 10b). Then drop the broken tablets into the bottle or tube all at the same time. Quickly push a rubber stopper firmly into the mouth of the bottle (see Figure 10c) and stand to one side. Do not stand near the mouth of the tube or bottle or point it at anyone!

The seltzer tablets react (fizz) with the water to form

carbon dioxide gas. The gas raises the pressure inside the bottle until it becomes so strong that it pops the rubber stopper out of the bottle. Which way does the stopper move? Which way did the bottle first move when the stopper popped out? What evidence of the third law of motion did you observe when the stopper popped out of the bottle?

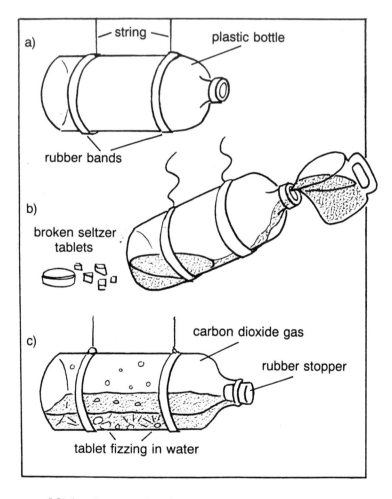

10) Another way to observe the third law of motion.

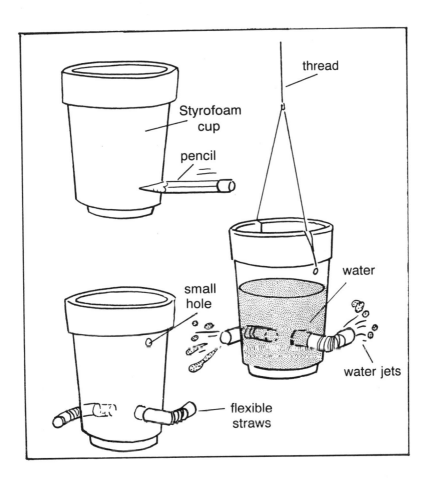

11) A rotating jet-powered cup fueled by water.

4. Build a rotating jet-powered cup, as shown in Figure 11. Use a sharp pencil to make two small holes on opposite sides near the bottom of a Styrofoam cup. Cut off the ends of two flexible plastic drinking straws and push their ends through the holes in the cup, as shown in Figure 11. Make two small holes on opposite sides near the top of the cup. Use two pieces of thread to suspend the cup over a sink. Fill the cup with water

and watch it turn as it reacts to the action of the water jetting from opposite sides of the cup.

Hold the end of the long thread and let the empty cup unwind. Now turn one of the straw jets around so that the water jets tend to turn the cup in opposite directions. What happens when you fill the cup with water and let the water flow from the straw jets this time?

PUZZLER 1.3

Return once more to our spaceship coasting through space. What could be done to make the spaceship go faster? What could be done to make it go slower?

The fastest humans can run at speeds of 43.4 kilometers (27 miles) per hour for short distances. By strapping on skates, they can reach speeds greater than 48.3 kilometers (30 miles) per hour. Using skis and the pull of gravity on a steep hill, they have exceeded 160.9 kilometers (100 miles) per hour. How fast can you run?

How Animals Move

Motion is one of the characteristics of living animals. Some animals move very fast; others are quite slow. Cheetahs can run at speeds as great as 117.6 kilometers (74 miles) per hour—fast enough to capture even the speedy pronghorn antelope, which can run at 88 kilometers (55 miles) per hour for about half a mile. On the other hand, a snail's pace is about 4.8/100 kilometer (3/100 mile) per hour. At this rate, a snail requires almost one and a half days to crawl 1.6 kilometers (or 1 mile). The fastest humans can run at speeds of about 12 meters (13 yards) per second (43 kilometers or 27 miles per hour) for short distances. By strapping skates to their feet, they can move quite a bit faster. Unlike other animals, humans have invented vehicles that can carry them at speeds as great as 40,000 kilometers (25,000 miles) per hour.

2.1   HUMANS IN MOTION

There is substantial evidence that our ancestors began walking upright on two legs millions of years ago. Our bigger brains came later. Being upright freed our hands for grasping and using tools—a development that gave us a great advantage over other animals in our quest for survival. We have, however, paid a price for our upright posture. Carrying all our weight on two legs places a lot of stress on the knee and hip joints. That is why surgeons are so busy replacing hip and knee joints in older people and repairing knee cartilage and ligaments in young athletes.

Walking

After our first year of life, walking is our most common form of locomotion. Once we learn to balance our bodies, we walk without giving it much thought. If you think about how you walk, you will realize that walking can be explained by Newton's laws of motion. To walk, you push backward and downward against the earth with your foot. The earth, as Newton's third law predicts, pushes your foot upward and forward. That force causes you to accelerate. A short time later, your other foot strikes the ground in front of you. This time, you push slightly forward as well as down against the earth. You receive an equal but opposite force from the earth that causes you to *decelerate* (reduce your speed). That same foot then pushes backward against the earth and the cycle is repeated again and again.

Running

Running is similar, but the forces tend to be larger and more frequent. When we run, our legs are bent more. Our feet strike the earth with a bigger force; our arched feet and stretched tendons act like springs. They compress as our feet strike the earth and then extend in a springlike fashion, helping us to "bounce" into our next stride.

2.2 WALKING ON A SLIPPERY EARTH

To do this experiment you will need:
- adult to help you
- several wooden dowels, metal rollers, or an old broom handle and saw
- short length of wide board
- smooth level ground

If you have ever walked on thick, loose sand, you know it is difficult. Your foot slides over the sand as you try to push backward against the earth. A similar, but more difficult experience occurs when you try to walk on ice. There is so little friction between your foot and the ice that you are unable to push against the earth. Your foot simply slips away and you fall.

You can experience something similar to walking on ice by placing a short, wide board on three or four wooden dowels or metal rollers on a smooth, level surface, as shown in Figure 12. (If you do not have dowels or rollers, you can make some by *asking an adult* to saw an old broom handle into three or four equal lengths.) *Ask an adult* to hold on to you. Then place one foot on the board and try to take a step forward with your other foot. What happens?

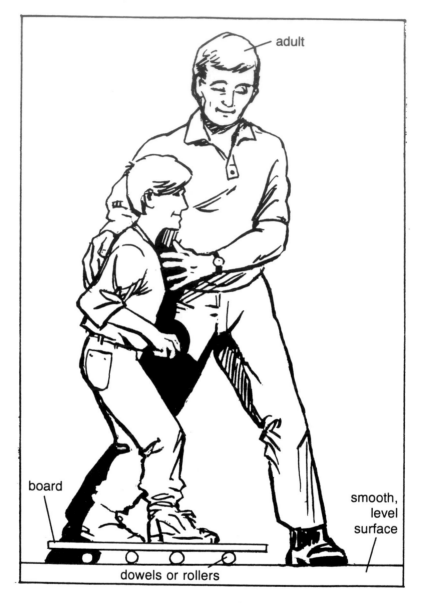

12) It's like walking on ice!

2.3   MUSCLES: THE SOURCE OF MOVEMENT

Like all animals, our ability to move depends on muscles. Muscles are attached to bones—the framework of our bodies. Muscles can contract and pull on bones, but they cannot push. This means that our muscles must come in pairs. One muscle, or set of muscles, bends a joint one way; the other member of the pair bends the joint the other way (see Figure 13).

To see how this works, place one hand on the upper part of your other arm—the part above your elbow. When you bend your arm upward, as you would to bring food to your mouth, you can feel the biceps muscle on the front side of your upper arm contract. Place your hand on the inside of your elbow as you bend your arm. You can feel the cordlike tendon that connects the biceps to your lower arm bone. To straighten your arm, you contract the triceps muscle on the backside of your arm. If you straighten your arm as much as you can, you will feel the triceps shorten and bulge on the back of your arm. Move your fingers to the tip of your elbow, and contract the muscle as tightly as you can. You will feel the tendon that connects the triceps to the elbow, which is the end of one of the two bones in your lower arm (the ulna).

A similar arrangement of muscles is used to bend

your leg. If you grasp the back of your leg as you bend it, you will feel your hamstring muscles contract. Place your hand behind the inside of your knee as you bend your leg. You can easily feel one of the large tendons that connects the muscle to the lower leg. The quadriceps muscles on the front side of your upper leg contract to straighten your leg. Feel those muscles shorten and bulge when you make your leg as straight as possible. You can also feel the tendons that attach these muscles to your lower leg. They run on either side of your knee cap.

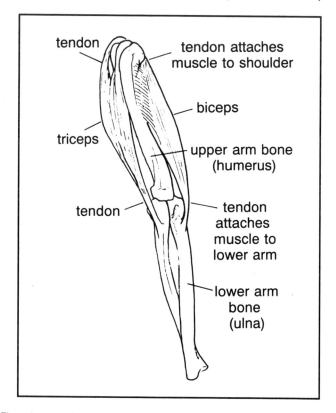

tendon

tendon attaches muscle to shoulder

biceps

triceps

upper arm bone (humerus)

tendon

tendon attaches muscle to lower arm

lower arm bone (ulna)

13) The two sets of muscles that bend the arm are the biceps and triceps. The biceps muscle is used to bend your arm. Contraction of the triceps muscle straightens your arm.

2.4   HOW FAST CAN YOU MOVE ALONG THE EARTH?

To do this experiment you will need:
- friend to help you
- ice-skating rink, if possible
- park, athletic field, or large lawn with smooth, level ground
- tape measure
- swimming pool, if possible
- stopwatch or watch with a second hand

Find a long stretch of smooth, level ground in a park, athletic field, or a large lawn. Measure off a 91.4-meter (100-yard) length with a tape measure. If you choose a football field, the distance from goal line to goal line is 91.4 meters (100 yards). Ask a friend to use a stopwatch or a watch with a second hand to time you as you walk the measured distance at your normal walking pace.

Determining Your Walking Speed

To find your walking speed, divide the distance you walked (300 feet) by the time it took you to walk that distance. For example, suppose you walked the 300 feet in 75 seconds. With a pocket calculator you can calculate your speed. It would be:

$$\frac{300 \text{ feet}}{75 \text{ seconds}} = 4.0 \text{ feet per second}$$

If you would like to know your speed in miles per hour (mph), simply multiply the speed in feet per second by 0.68 because 1 foot per second is the same as 0.68 miles per hour.

4.0 feet per second x 0.68 miles per hour = 2.7 miles per hour.

What is your friend's walking speed in feet per second and in miles per hour? Repeat the experiment, but this time, run as fast as you can. What is your fastest running speed in feet per second and in miles per hour? How fast can your friend run?

If possible, find an ice-skating rink and measure your speed on skates. How fast can you skate? How fast can your friend skate?

Next time you go swimming, measure your swimming speed. How fast can you swim? How fast can your friend swim?

Table 5 contains some record winning times in running, speed skating, and swimming events. How fast did each record holder run, skate, or swim? How do their speeds compare with yours?

TABLE 5:
RECORD-WINNING TIMES IN RUNNING, SPEED SKATING, AND SWIMMING EVENTS.

Winner (seconds)	Event	Distance (meters)	(feet)	Time (seconds)
Carl Lewis	running	100	328	9.86
Dan Jansen	speed skating	500	1,640	36.02
Matt Biondi	freestyle swimming	100	328	48.63

2.5   HORSES IN MOTION

Your leg has two main parts that make up most of its length. The femur is your upper leg bone. Your tibia (or shin bone) and the smaller fibula, which lies beside the tibia, are the two bones in your lower leg (see Figure 14a). A horse's leg is given added length by a third bone—the cannon. It consists of two bones found in the feet of other animals, including yourself, that have

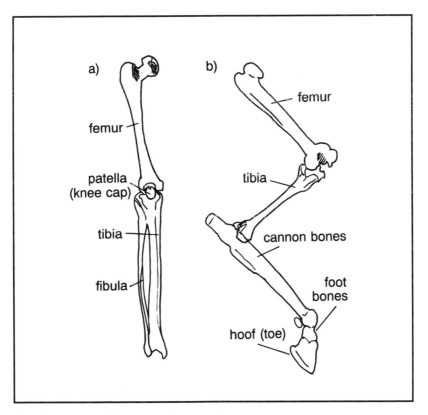

14a) Upper and lower leg bones of a human.

b) Rear leg of a horse. The bones of the foot and ankle fuse to form the cannon, which gives the horse an additional joint in its leg.

fused and lengthened. As a result, horses actually run on their hooves (see Figure 14b).

A horse runs at three speeds, or gaits. When walking, a horse moves one foot at a time. The feet move in a regular order: right fore foot, left hind foot, left fore foot, right hind foot, as shown in Figure 15a. A trotting horse moves at about 16 kilometers (10 miles) per hour, three times faster than a walking horse. In this gait, the fore leg on one side of the body moves forward at the same time as the hind leg on the other side of the body. Some horses are pacers. Like camels and some dogs with long legs, they move both the hind leg and the fore leg on the same side of the body forward at the same time.

The horse's fastest gait is the gallop. In a gallop (see Figure 15b), a horse pulls its hind legs under its body and then pushes off with great force as its rear leg muscles push its hooves downward and backward against the ground. In each galloping stride, all four feet are off the ground at one point. When the fore legs strike the ground, the back bends. The hindquarters are brought forward and the rear feet strike the ground. As the horse pushes off its rear feet, its back straightens, pushing the forequarters farther forward than would be the case if its back had not been bent.

Like human runners, horses also store energy in their tendons as their hooves strike the earth. This stored energy is released as the animals rebound and accelerate.

Calculating Horses' Speeds

At the Kentucky Derby, horses run on a track that is 2.0 kilometers (1.25 miles) long. The race takes just about 2 minutes. What is the average speed of the horses in miles per minute and in miles per hour?

At the Belmont Stakes, the track is 2.4 kilometers (1.5 miles) long. The horses run this race in about 2.5 minutes. How does the speed of the horses in this event compare with their speed in the Kentucky Derby?

The fastest humans can run a mile in a little under 4 minutes. How do the running speeds of the fastest horses and humans compare?

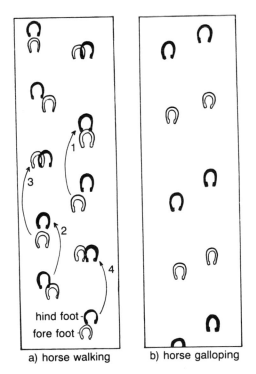

15) A horse's hoofprints while: a) walking; b) galloping.

2.6   SLITHERING SNAKES

As you know, snakes do not have legs. A snake placed on a very smooth floor cannot move because there is not enough friction. Snakes move by using their muscles to form their bodies into an *S* or similar wavy shape. Their muscles then contract along the waves pushing the body forward. As this happens, the snake's head moves forward, forming a new wave, while its forward-moving tail leaves waves behind.

How Snakes Move

To better understand how a snake moves, think of one curved section of a snake as your bent forearm. By pushing your forearms downward onto the arms of a chair you can lift your body out of the chair. A snake moves in a similar way except that it moves horizontally by pushing its body against the ground (see Figure 16a).

On loose sand, many snakes, including rattlesnakes, use a sidewinding motion like that shown in Figure 16b. Instead of pushing against the sand, which gives way, the snake lifts its body section by section and moves to a new place. Its previous positions are left as tracks in the sand.

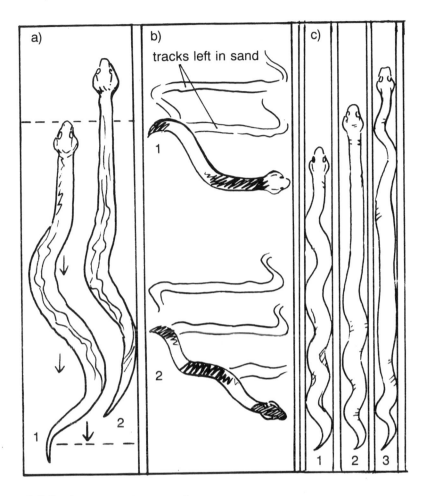

16) Snakes move in several ways.

a) They can form waves in their bodies and push forward. This is called *serpentine motion*. The arrows show where the snake's body pushes against the ground.

b) On loose sand, many snakes move by *sidewinding*. In the drawings, the darker parts of the snake represent parts that are in the sand. The lighter segments are parts the snake has lifted off the ground.

c) *Concertina* locomotion enables snakes to move along narrow openings. In (1) and (2), pleats are unfolding, moving the snake forward. In (3), new pleats are forming as old ones are "pressed" out.

To climb trees or move through narrow openings (fissures) in rocks, snakes fold their bodies into pleats like an accordion. Called *concertina locomotion*, this wedges the curled parts of the snake's body tightly against the grooves in the bark or rock. The friction prevents the snake's body from sliding backward as it extends the front of its body forward (see Figure 16c).

Most snakes do not move very fast. The fastest snake, the black mamba, can move at about 11 kilometers (7 miles) per hour, but only for short periods of time.

2.7   CRAWLING LIKE A SNAKE

To do this experiment you will need:
- carpeted floor
- smooth, uncarpeted floor

Lie on one side on a carpeted floor. Bend your legs. Now, try to move forward by straightening your legs. Then, lift your shoulder and move your upper body forward. Bend your legs and repeat the motion. Can you crawl along the floor on your side? Is this similar to the way a snake moves? How is it different? Now, repeat the experiment on a smooth floor, such as a linoleum or smooth-tiled floor. What do you find?

If possible, watch a snake in a zoo as it moves. If nonpoisonous snakes are a common sight around your home, watch them as they move. If there are poisonous snakes near your home, **ask an adult** to identify any snake you see before you stay to watch it move.

2.8   OTHER CRAWLING ANIMALS

To do this experiment you will need:
- earthworms
- snails
- caterpillars
- slugs

Watch other animals such as earthworms, caterpillars, snails, and slugs as they crawl. How do their methods of crawling compare with the way snakes move?

Mark the position of one or more of these crawling animals. Then, use a stopwatch or a watch with a second hand to see how far the animal moves in 2 minutes. What is the animal's speed in feet per minute, in inches per minute, and in inches per second?

PUZZLER 2.3
How can you find the animal's speed in miles per hour?

2.9   BIRDS AND FLIGHT

What Animals Need in Order to Fly

More than wings are required for an animal to fly. Birds are able to fly because of several reasons. One reason is that they digest and "burn" (metabolize) their food rapidly. This gives them the power needed to fly, that is, the ability to produce lots of energy every second. Bats and flying insects have the same ability to produce power.

Oxygen makes up about 1/5 of the air we and other animals breathe. Animals obtain oxygen from the air or, in the case of fish, from oxygen dissolved in water. To burn food rapidly, an animal requires an abundance of oxygen. In addition to lungs, birds have air sacs connected to their lungs. These sacs increase the amount of oxygen available to the blood. They also have strong hearts that beat rapidly, carrying oxygen-rich blood and food to the birds' muscles.

The birds' air sacs, together with their thin, hollow bones, help to make them lighter than other animals of the same size. Their light weight makes it easier for them to overcome gravity, as they must, in order to fly. The breeding of birds such as chickens and domestic turkeys has been controlled by humans in order to increase the amount of meat on their bodies. These birds are no longer able to fly very far—they are simply too heavy.

The muscles that control a bird's wings are found on the animal's chest, not on its wing bones the way our arm muscles are located on our arms. Birds have long tendons that extend from the muscles on their chests to their wing bones. These long tendons allow birds to flap their wings without having to move their muscles through the same distances that the wings travel. When we move our arms up and down, the muscles in our arms move as far as our arms. If birds had to move muscles in their wings, as well as the bones, skin, and feathers there, they would not be able to fly much farther than you can. Other adaptations that birds have for flying include a small, light head that lacks teeth and the muscles necessary to use them.

How Birds Fly

To fly, a bird keeps its wing turned to provide an angle much like that of an airplane, as shown in Figure 17. The air deflected downward by the wing provides an upward force. Such an angle of attack is helpful for birds that soar.

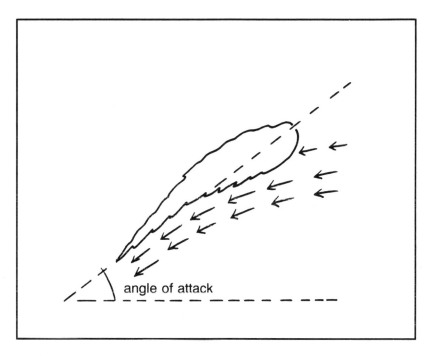

angle of attack

17) A bird, like an airplane, keeps its wing at an angle of attack that forces air downward. Newton's third law tells us that the bird will receive an upward force from the deflected air.

During flight, a bird's wings move in the manner shown in Figure 18. On the downstroke, the feathers push air downward and backward. From Newton's third law of motion, we know that the bird will receive a force that pushes it upward and forward. On the upstroke, the wing is bent to reduce the area that pushes against the air. By reducing the wing's area as it rises, the downward

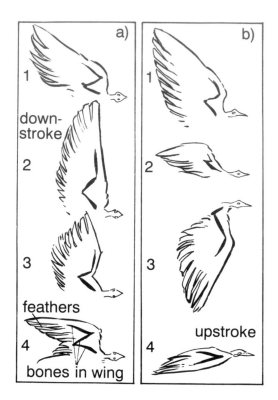

18) A bird's wing during flight as seen at four different stages:
a) from above; b) from the side.

force on the bird is lessened. The downward force is also reduced during the upstroke by "feathering" the larger wing feathers—the feathers separate and turn edgewise so that air can flow between them.

Birds can move at high speeds. Swifts, which are appropriately named, have been clocked at speeds exceeding 160 kilometers (100 miles) per hour. Diving eagles and hawks have been followed by airplanes at speeds of 290 kilometers (180 miles) per hour. Birds can also fly great distances. During spring and fall migrations, they often travel several thousand miles.

2.10 CHICKEN AND MAMMAL BONES

To do this experiment you will need:
- adult to help you
- bones from chickens, turkeys, fish, cows (steaks), pigs (chops, ribs, and roasts)
- old newspapers
- water
- large cooking pot
- stove
- saw

You are probably used to finding bones when you eat chicken, but steaks, chops, ribs, and roasts often have bones as well. Save these bones. **Ask an adult** to help you boil the bones in a pot of hot water. After the bones have cooled, pull away any remaining meat and gristle with your fingers. Lay the bones on some old newspapers for a couple of days until they are thoroughly dry.

You can probably break dry chicken bones with your fingers. What do you notice about the inside of a chicken or turkey bone? What do you notice about the thickness of a chicken or turkey bone? Are chicken and turkey bones flexible?

To compare a bird bone (chicken or turkey) with a mammal bone (cow or pig), **ask an adult** to use a saw to cut across a mammal bone. How does the inside of a mammal bone compare with the inside of a bird bone? Which bone is more flexible? Which bone is hollow?

2.11   NATURAL SWIMMERS

You can swim, but it is not your natural means of loco-motion. For fish and mammals that live in the sea, swimming is their means of locomotion. Like most mammals, some fish are denser than water. (Their bod-ies weigh more than an equal volume of water.) Some of these fish are bottom dwellers. Others, such as sharks, use their fins and tails to constantly push downward on the water. The water, in return (Newton's third law of mo-tion), provides an upward force. The flesh and livers of many fish are rich in fats and oils, which reduce the density of their bodies. Some fish have what is called a swim bladder—a gas-filled bladder that lies along the upper side of their bodies. As a fish moves downward in water, the pressure on its body increases and the swim bladder becomes smaller. This causes the fish to lose buoyancy and sink. However, these fish are able to add gas to the bladder. Gases dissolved in their blood move slowly into the swim bladder. On the other hand, as a fish rises in the water, the pressure on its body de-creases. The swim bladder tends to expand and make the fish float to the surface. But chemical changes within a fish's body cause the gas in its swim bladder to dissolve in its blood as the pressure decreases.

How Fish Swim

Fish have streamlined bodies that move through the water with very little friction. The muscles that drive the tail provide the main force that pushes a fish forward. The large tail fin (see Figure 19a) can push a lot of water as it moves from side to side, but it also pushes water backward (see Figure 19b). From Newton's third law, we know that the water that is pushed backward will push the fish forward. Of course, the fish is also pushed to one side as well. However, because it moves its tail from one side to the other, the side pushes cancel each other. When the tail moves forward, as it must before it can sweep water backward, the tail fin turns so as to push as little water as possible forward (see Figure

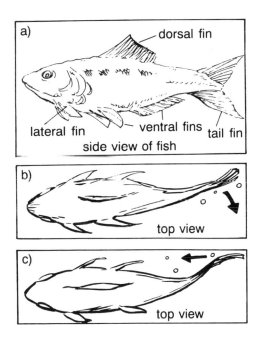

19a) A fish's tail fin, as you can see, is quite wide.

b) By pushing its tail fin back against the water, a fish propels itself forward.

c) The tail has to move forward before it can push water backward. During its forward motion, the fin is turned so as to push against as little water as possible.

19c). Fish can also use their lateral (side), dorsal (top), and ventral (lower) fins (see Figure 19a) for stability and to move slowly backward, forward, up, down, or sideways.

Mammals That Swim

Whales and dolphins propel themselves through water in a way that is similar to the locomotion of fish. However, their tails, as shown in Figure 20, move up and down rather than from side to side. Their movements resemble a giant fish turned on its side. But whales and dolphins are not fish; they are mammals that live in the sea. They have lungs, not gills. They breathe air through a blowhole on the top of their head, and they bear live young (they do not lay eggs like fish do). Whales will drown if they cannot rise to the surface to breathe.

20) The up and down motion of a bottlenose dolphin's tail provides the force that drives the animal through the water. If you have seen dolphins perform, you know that they swim very fast and can propel their bodies to great heights above the water.

The Speed of Fish

In general, fish are not rapid swimmers. Most of them cannot swim faster than 8 kilometers (5 miles) per hour. Tuna are quite fast and have been known to swim at speeds of 32 kilometers (20 miles) per hour or faster. Barracudas are probably the fastest fish. Four-foot-long fish of this species have been clocked at speeds of 44 kilometers (27 miles) per hour.

Bottlenose dolphins can swim at about 32 kilometers (20 miles) per hour, and killer whales (orcas) can reach speeds of 48 kilometers (30 miles) per hour. Whaling ships used to search the seas for "right whales." This species of whale (see Figure 21) was so named because whalers said they were the "right" whales to hunt. The

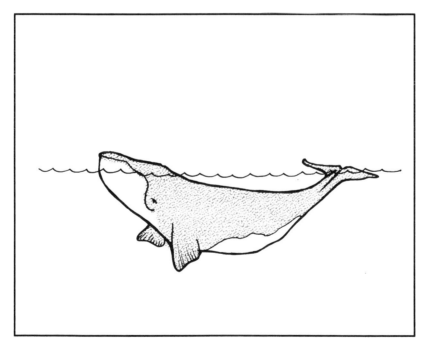

21) The right whale is an endangered species.

animals were gentle, unafraid, lived close to shore, and could move no faster than 10 kilometers (6 miles) per hour. Their bodies were so filled with oils that they floated after being killed. By the middle of the eighteenth century, these easy-to-harpoon whales were seldom seen in the whaling waters around New England. Although protected from further whaling, they remain an endangered species.

PUZZLER 2.4
How do the speeds of fish compare with the speed of a champion human swimmer? (See Table 5.)

2.12   FISH BONES

To do this experiment you will need:
- adult to help you
- cooked fish
- warm, running water

Next time you have fish for dinner, take a look at its skeleton. You will need a whole fish, such as a herring, mackerel, or perch. After the fish has been cooked, **ask an adult** to cut away the flesh, leaving the skeleton. You can clean the skeleton in warm, running water.

Look at the backbone. It is made up of a number of smaller bones called vertebrae. How many vertebrae are in the fish's backbone? Bend the backbone from side to side. Notice how flexible it is. The vertebrae can move along the joints that separate them from one another. What else does a fish use when it moves?

2.13 HOW OILS HELP KEEP FISH FROM SINKING

To do this experiment you will need:
- water
- clear plastic cup
- cooking oil

This experiment will help you to see why flesh and livers rich in fats and oils help to keep fish from sinking in water the way you do. Half-fill a clear, plastic cup with water. Then, carefully pour a small amount of cooking oil into the water. Does the cooking oil sink or float in water?

Something that is denser than water (weighs more than an equal volume of water) will sink in water. Is cooking oil more or less dense than water? How can you tell?

The fastest speed for the Indianapolis 500 is 299.2 kilometers (185.9 miles) per hour. It was set by Arie Luyendyk in 1990. The fastest 1.6 kilometer (1 mile) speed in a jet-powered car is 1,019.5 kilometers (633.6 miles) per hour. However, these speeds pale in comparison with the 40,225 kilometers (25,000 miles) per hour maximum velocities attained by the spaceships that traveled to the moon during the 1960s and 1970s.

Vehicles That Stop and Go

We travel from place to place in many different kinds of vehicles—cars, trucks, trains, boats, airplanes—everything from skateboards to space shuttles. To be of any use, these vehicles must be able to stop as well as go. In this chapter, we will look at how vehicles stop and go. Since a bicycle is probably your most common means of locomotion other than walking, we will start there.

3.1 HOW BICYCLES GO

To do this experiment you will need:
- bicycle with three or more speeds
- smooth, level path or sidewalk

To make your bicycle go, you push on the pedals. A chain connects the gear (sprocket) that is attached to the pedals to a gear that is attached to the bike's rear wheel, as shown in Figure 22. In bicycles that have more than one speed, you can shift the chain so that it connects different gears. See if you can figure out how the chain is moved from one gear to another. Some multispeed bikes have one gear that turns with the pedals and three that turn with the rear wheel. Most ten-speed bikes have two gears connected to the pedals and five to the rear wheel. Eighteen-speed bikes usually have three gears that turn with the pedals and six with the rear wheel.

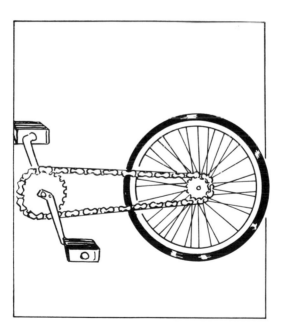

22) A chain connects the sprocket to the gear on the rear wheel.

Shifting Gears

Take your bike on a short ride. During the ride, shift gears until the chain is on the largest gear connected to the pedals and the largest gear connected to the rear wheel. Now, turn the bike upside down. Slowly turn the pedal with your hand. Count the number of times the rear wheel goes around when you turn the pedal around once. The easiest way to count the turns of the rear wheel is to watch the valve stem. If the wheel turns too fast, hold it gently with your hand so it does not turn freely. How many times does the wheel go around when the pedals make one complete turn? How many teeth are on the gear connected to the pedals? How many teeth are on the large gear that turns with the rear wheel?

Take your bike on another short ride. This time, shift gears until the chain is on the largest gear connected to the pedals and the smallest gear connected to the rear wheel. Turn the bike upside down again and re-peat the experiment. How many times does the wheel go around when the pedals make one complete turn? How many teeth are on the gear connected to the pedals? How many teeth are on the small gear that turns with the rear wheel?

With which of the two arrangements of gears you have tested is the bicycle easier to pedal? Which gear arrangement would you use to pedal up a hill? Which would you use to go fast along a level bike path?

To see how different gear connections affect the speed of a bike, look at the gears in Figure 23. How many teeth does gear 1 have? How many teeth does gear 2 have? When gear 1 makes one complete turn, how many turns does gear 2 make? If a wheel, such as a bicycle wheel, were attached to gear 2, how many turns would it make when gear 1, attached to the pedals, made one turn?

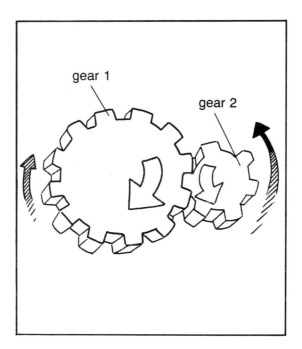

gear 1

gear 2

23) Gear 1 and gear 2 are meshed so that when one turns, so does the other.

The force that makes your bike go comes from your foot pushing on the pedals. Take your bike to a smooth, level path or sidewalk. Starting from rest with one of the bike's pedals at its highest point, push on that pedal with your foot through half a turn to make your bike go. What happens to your bike's speed as you push on the pedal? Repeat the experiment, but this time, push harder on the pedal. How does your acceleration compare with your acceleration when you did not push as hard? Which of Newton's laws apply to this experiment?

PUZZLER 3.1
If the gear connected to the pedals of a bicycle meshed with the gear connected to the rear wheel (see Figures 22 and 23), would the wheel turn in the same direction as the pedals or in the opposite direction? What is one advantage of using a chain to link the two gears on a bicycle?

3.2   HOW BICYCLES STOP

To do this experiment you will need:
- bicycle
- smooth, level path
  or sidewalk
- stick
- level lawn
- bicycle tire pump

One way to stop your bike is to apply the brakes. If you have hand brakes, the brake pads push on the rims of the wheels. If you have a coaster brake and push backward on a pedal to stop, the brake rubs against the wheel's hub. In either case, friction is applied to the wheels until they stop turning.

Applying the Brakes!

What happens if you do not apply your brakes? Will it coast forever? Take your bicycle to a smooth, level path or sidewalk. Use a stick to mark a starting point on the path. Place the front wheel of the bike on the mark.

Starting from rest, with one of the bike's pedals at its highest point, push on the pedal through half a turn to make your bike go. Continue to coast on the bike until it stops. How far did you go? (You can measure the distance by counting the number of paces back to your starting point.)

Repeat the experiment on a level lawn. How far do you coast when you do this experiment on a lawn? Was there more friction on the lawn or on the hard-surfaced path or sidewalk? How do you know?

This experiment also demonstrates Newton's second law of motion. But, in which direction does the force push on the bike as it coasts along the lawn or path? What happens to the bike's speed as it coasts along the level surfaces? If there were no friction on the bike as it coasted on a level surface, how far would it travel?

Repeat the experiment on a smooth, level path or sidewalk once more. How far did you travel this time? Now let some air out of the bike tires until they are quite soft. Repeat the experiment with soft tires. How far did you coast with the soft tires? Was there more friction on the soft tires or on the hard tires? How can you tell? (Don't forget to use a bicycle tire pump to pump the tires back to their original pressure.)

3.3   HOW CARS STOP AND GO

The energy that moves most cars comes from burning gasoline. The gasoline burns very fast (you might say it explodes) inside a cylinder and drives a piston along the cylinder. There are usually several pistons in a car's engine, each of which is connected to a crankshaft. Gasoline vapor is injected into the cylinder and a spark plug ignites the fumes. The order in which the fuel is ignited is fixed so that the crankshaft turns smoothly. The crankshaft is connected through a series of gears to the wheels.

To stop a car, the driver pushes on a brake pedal. The pedal is connected through levers and hydraulic fluid to brake pads. When the pedal is pushed, brake pads rub against discs connected to the wheels, as shown in Figure 24. Friction between the pads and the discs slows the discs and the wheels to which they are

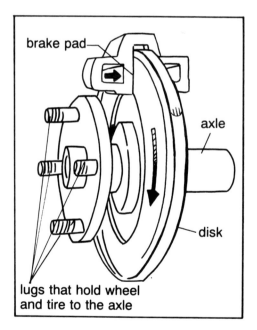

24) Pressure from hydraulic fluid pushes the brake pad against a disk that is connected to the car's wheel. The disk is exposed to air so that the heat produced by the brake pads rubbing on the disk can be carried away by the cooler air.

attached. In most cars, the brake pads on the front wheels touch the discs before those on the rear wheels. The next experiment will help you to see why.

3.4   CARS, BRAKES, AND ICY ROADS

To do this experiment you will need:
- toy car or truck with wheels that turn freely
- large, shallow tray (such as a cafeteria tray)
- water
- long, wide, smooth board
- ruler
- rubber band
- freezer

Place a toy car or truck on a long, wide, smooth board. How high do you have to lift one end of the board before the toy vehicle rolls down the "hill"? You can use a ruler to measure the height of the end of the board. The higher you lift the board, the greater is the part of the force of gravity that pulls the vehicle along the board. You know from your own experience on a bike or sled that the pull of gravity is greater on a steep hill than on a slight incline.

Making Brakes

Wrap a rubber band around the front wheels of the toy vehicle, as shown in Figure 25. The rubber band acts like brakes applied to the front wheels. Now, how high do you have to lift the end of the board before the vehicle rolls down the hill?

Repeat the experiment, but this time wrap the rubber band around the rear wheels. How high do you have to lift the end of the board before the vehicle moves down the hill? What happens to the vehicle as it goes down the hill this time? Why are cars made so that brakes are applied to the front wheels before the rear ones? Place the toy car or truck on a large, shallow tray, such as a cafeteria tray. How high do you have to lift one end of the tray before the toy vehicle rolls down the hill? Apply the rubber band to the front wheels as you did earlier. Now, how high do you have to lift the board before the vehicle slides? Record that height on a piece of paper.

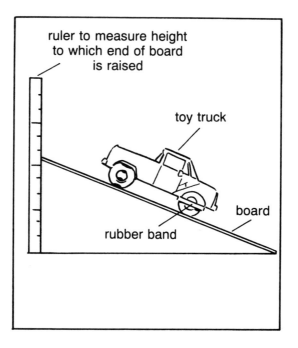

ruler to measure height
to which end of board
is raised

toy truck

board

rubber band

25) A rubber band acts as a brake on the wheels of a toy vehicle.

Brakes on Ice

Place the tray in a freezer. Be sure that it is level. Then pour water into the tray until it is covered with a thin layer of the liquid. Leave the tray in the freezer for several hours until the water is completely frozen.

Remove the tray from the freezer and place it on a level table or counter. Put the toy vehicle with its braked front wheels on the tray. How high do you have to lift the board before the vehicle slides? How does ice affect the friction between the vehicle and the surface along which it moves? What do you predict will happen if you put the brakes on the rear wheels and then raise the end of the tray? Try it with the vehicle at an angle, as shown in Figure 26. Was your prediction correct? Now, try it with braked front wheels and the vehicle at an angle. What is different when the vehicle starts to slide this time?

3.5   HOW BOATS STOP AND GO

All water-going vessels, be they large or small, share one common characteristic. They all weigh less than an equal volume of water; that is, they are less dense than water. To propel canoes and rowboats, people use paddles or oars. The paddle or oar pushing water backward receives an equal push forward from the water—another example of Newton's third law of motion.

Using Propellers in Water

Aside from sailboats, which rely on wind for motion, most vessels that carry passengers are powered by

top view of toy vehicle on tray

slowly lift this
end of tray

ice

tray

26) With brakes on the back wheels, place the vehicle at an
angle on the ice-covered tray. What will happen when
the tray becomes a "hill"?

rotating propellers. In small powerboats, the propellers
are driven by gasoline engines. In large oceangoing
passenger ships, they are turned by steam turbines. Regardless of how they are powered, these propellers
push water backward. The water, in turn, pushes the
ship forward. Smaller propellers are used to push the
ship sideways during docking or when traveling through
narrow passages.

Rudders are used to steer boats. The rudder can be

turned so that it deflects water to the right or left. If water is deflected to the left, as shown in Figure 27, the boat will turn to the left. Notice that the rudder handle is turned to the right.

If you have ever tried to run in waist-deep water, you know that it is not difficult to make a boat decelerate. With the propeller turned off, friction between the boat and the water quickly reduces the boat's speed. However, it is possible to reverse the direction of rotation of the propeller that drives the ship. When that is done, it will push water forward and the water will push the ship backward.

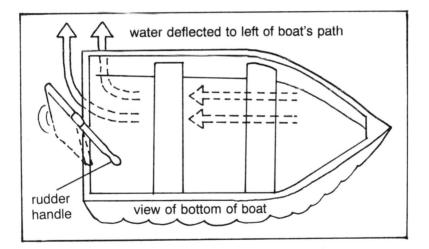

water deflected to left of boat's path

rudder handle

view of bottom of boat

27) If the rudder deflects water to the left, which way will the boat turn?

3.6 METAL BOATS

To do this experiment you will need:
- sheet of aluminum foil
- sink
- water

If all boats are less dense than water, how can ships be made of steel? (During World War II, some ships were made of concrete.) You can answer this question by tightly folding a sheet of aluminum foil into a small square or rectangle. Partially fill a sink with water. Drop the folded aluminum into the water and watch it sink. Remove the aluminum and unfold it. Then fold it into the shape of a boat. Be sure to seal the front and rear edges so water cannot enter the boat. Place the boat back in the water. As you can see, the boat floats even though it is made of aluminum, which is nearly three times as dense as water.

> **PUZZLER 3.2**
> Why will a boat float even when it is made of material that is denser than water?

3.7 A PROPELLER

To do this experiment you will need:
- adult to help you
- electric fan

Look at an electric fan. You can see that it has a propeller. The propeller is turned by an electric motor that is attached to it. **Ask an adult** to help you connect the fan to an electric outlet. **Do not put your hands** *close to the fan,* but feel the air coming from the fan. Which way is the fan pushing the air? Which way is the air pushing the fan? You can feel the air moving. Why doesn't the fan move in the opposite direction?

3.8 HOW AIRPLANES STOP AND GO Using Propellers in Air

Before jet airplanes were developed, all airplanes had propellers. The propellers pushed the air backward and received an equal reaction force that pushed the plane forward. This force accelerated the airplane until air rushing against the wing at a proper angle of attack was able to lift the plane off the ground (see Experiment 2.9). The propeller then continued to drive the plane forward, while air rushing against the wing provided the upward push needed to overcome gravity.

Reducing the rate at which the propeller turned would slow the airplane. Flaplike structures (rudders, elevators, and ailerons) on the tail and wings could be lowered or turned to control the plane's direction and make it tip, turn, climb, or descend. These structures deflect air in the same way that a ship's rudder deflects water. The effect is the same. By deflecting air, the plane can be made to turn, tip, rise, or drop. After landing, brakes can be applied to the wheels to make the plane stop.

Using Jet Engines in Air

Today, most passengers fly in planes powered by jet engines. Rudders, elevators, and ailerons are still used to control the plane, but the main force driving the plane is the jet engine. As you can see from Figure 28, air is pulled into the engine with a large fan. The air is then warmed by compression. It is warmed further by burning fuel before it enters the narrow exhaust where it leaves the engines at very high speed. The air forced out the exhaust exerts a very large forward force on the engine and the plane to which it is attached. This large force, another example of Newton's third law, is similar to the action-reaction effect you saw in Experiment 1.7

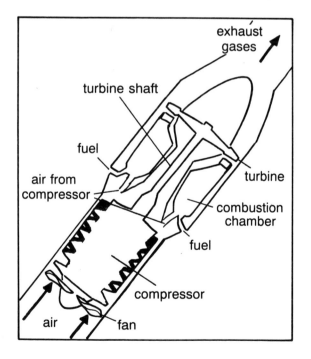

28) A cross section of a jet engine.

(where you observed an oblong balloon being driven forward as it forced air through its neck, or where you saw a plastic bottle spring forward as a rubber stopper popped out of the bottle's mouth). There is enough power in these jet engines to turn a turbine as well. The turbine provides the energy needed to operate the plane's many electrical and mechanical systems.

Using Jet Propulsion in Water

Squid often move by means of jet propulsion. They can squeeze water out of their body through a funnel-like tube. Like a jet airplane, the squid move in a direction opposite that in which the water is squirted. The tube can be directed forward or backward. Consequently, they can use jet propulsion to move in either direction.

3.9   INTO SPACE ON ROCKET SHIPS

Jet engines cannot work in the airless environment of space, but rocket engines, like the one shown in Figure 29, can be used to power spaceships. The rocket burns fuel that leaves the vehicle through the narrow exhaust. As the rocket pushes the burning fuel backwards through the exhaust, the burning fuel pushes the ship forward.

A Space Shuttle's Orbit

The space shuttle is carried into space by the giant rockets shown in Figure 30. Once in orbit around the earth, the shuttle can be maneuvered by means of small rockets on the ship. No fuel is required to keep the shuttle or any other satellite moving. The pull of gravity

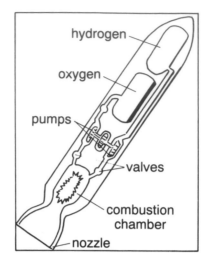

29) In this rocket engine, hydrogen burns in oxygen to produce water vapor at a very high temperature. The hot gases pushed out of the nozzle exert an equal force that drives the rocket forward.

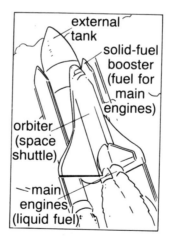

30) The space shuttle blasts off on a trip into orbit. The external tank provides the fuel needed to power the main engines on the ship. The solid fuel boosters provide additional power. Both the external tank and boosters are released and fall back to earth when emptied. Only the orbiter enters outer space.

together with the high speed of the orbiting satellite (about 29,000 kilometers or 18,000 miles per hour) keeps it in orbit.

If the shuttle were not moving, it would fall straight toward the earth, as shown in Figure 31a. If it were moving and there was no gravity, the shuttle would continue to move off into space along a straight line at constant speed, as shown in Figure 31b. Since it is moving and gravity does pull it toward earth, it follows the

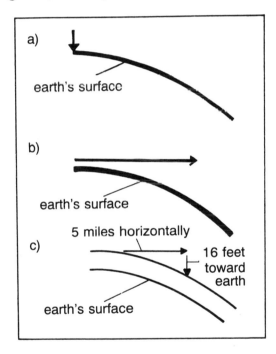

31a) If the space shuttle had no speed, it would fall straight down toward the earth.

b) If the space shuttle had a velocity and there was no gravity, it would move along a straight line into space.

c) The shuttle's actual path is the combination of its velocity and its fall due to gravity. The result is a curved path around the earth.

path shown in Figure 31c. In one second, the shuttle would travel about 8 kilometers (5 miles) horizontally. During that same second, it would fall 5 meters (16 feet) towards the earth. The sum of those two motions gives the curved orbit shown. If its orbit is circular, its curved path matches the earth's curvature.

Weightlessness

Everything on the shuttle is falling toward the earth at the same rate. This produces what is called *weightlessness*. Because the ship and everything in it are falling toward earth at the same rate, the ship's floor does not push on the astronauts' feet and their feet do not push on the floor. They float freely in the cabin. You feel weightless for a very short time when you jump from a chair to the floor. The astronauts riding in the space shuttle have this sensation of weightlessness all the time they are in orbit.

Returning to Earth

To return to earth, the space shuttle fires retro-rockets. That is, it shoots exhaust gases in the direction it is moving. The result is a force that opposes the ship's motion and causes it to decelerate. Although its speed decreases, the pull of gravity does not change. Consequently, the ship's path becomes more curved and it begins to move closer and closer to earth. Finally, it enters the atmosphere where the air pushes against it and slows it before it lands.

The space shuttle glides to a landing. By the time it reenters the earth's atmosphere, it has very little fuel left. Small adjustments in the ship's speed and direction can be made with the numerous small rockets that are located around the fuselage, but its path to a landing is primarily as a gliding heavier-than-air ship.

3.10 ROUND AND ROUND, DOWN AND DOWN WITH GRAVITY

To do this experiment you will need:
- marble
- plastic cover (the kind found on a frozen whipped topping container will work well)
- water
- scissors
- pencil
- Styrofoam cup
- plastic pail
- sink

A Marble Spaceship

You can make a model of a spaceship in orbit about the earth. A marble can be used to represent the spaceship. The rim of a plastic cover can supply the "gravity" that pulls the spaceship inward and keeps it in orbit. The center of the cover represents the earth. Give the marble a push so that it rolls around the model orbit, as shown in Figure 32a.

What would happen if there were no gravity pulling the ship toward the earth? To find out, use scissors to trim away several inches of the cover's edge (see Figure 32b). Which of the three paths shown in Figure 32c will the spaceship (marble) follow when there is no gravity (cover's edge) to guide it?

As you learned in Experiment 3.9, a spaceship in orbit around the earth is pulled toward the earth's center by gravity. In fact, as you have just seen, it is the force of gravity that keeps the ship from following a straight-line path out into space. Because a spaceship moves horizontally at nearly 29,000 kilometers (18,000 miles) per hour as it falls toward earth, the ship follows a curved orbit.

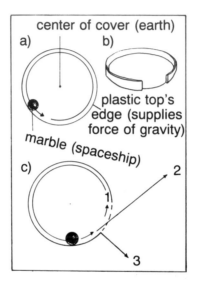

32a) A marble rolling around the inside edge of a plastic cover serves as a model of a spaceship orbiting the earth.

  b) Use scissors to trim away several inches of the cover's edge.

  c) If gravity is removed (the edge of the cover is cut away), will the "space shuttle" follow path 1, 2, or 3?

Creating a Circular Orbit

Pour some water into a plastic pail. Hold the pail above a sink and turn the pail upside down. You were not a bit surprised when the water fell from the pail. Now add water to the pail again. To feel the inward force that

78

keeps an object moving in a circular orbit, go outside and swing the pail in a' circle, as shown in Figure 33. You can feel your arm supplying the force that keeps the pail and contents moving in a circle.

Because the pail is moving fast enough, the water stays in the pail. Like a spaceship in orbit, the water moves horizontally as it falls. At the top of its orbit, water would fall from the pail if it were not moving. But it is moving. And, by the time it would have fallen some distance downward, it has moved along the circle to a position that is at least as far below the top of the circle as the water would have fallen. Consequently, the water stays in the pail just as you stay on the seat of a roller coaster when it is upside down during a loop-the-loop.

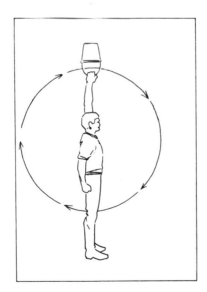

33) Your arm provides the force needed to keep the pail of water moving along a circular "orbit."

Testing Weightlessness

Astronauts in a spaceship orbiting the earth are weightless. The spaceship and all its contents are falling toward earth at the same rate. To see an effect of weightlessness, fill a Styrofoam cup with water. Hold the cup over a sink and use a sharp pencil to make a small hole in the side of the cup near the bottom, as shown in Figure 34. You can see a stream of water flowing from the cup. But suppose the cup were accelerating toward the earth at the same rate as the water in it. Would water still flow from the cup? To find out, fill the cup so that a stream flows out the hole in the side. Hold the cup high above a sink or

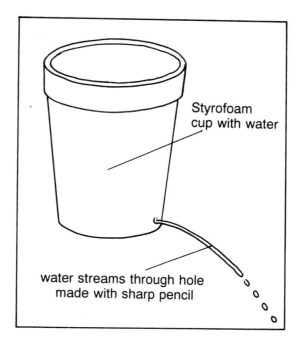

Styrofoam
cup with water

water streams through hole
made with sharp pencil

34) What will happen to the water stream if the cup is allowed to fall?

outside above the ground. If you drop the cup, will the cup and the water both accelerate toward the earth at the same rate? Do you think water will continue to flow from the cup? Try it! Were you right?

SURPRISE 3.1
Why did water stop flowing from the cup while the cup was falling?

3.11   PARACHUTES AND GLIDERS

To do this experiment you will need:
- thread
- metal washer
- other items you may want to use in making your own paper models of gliders
- large handkerchief
- paper
- plastic drinking straw
- tape
- scissors

As the spaceship lands, a parachute is released at the tail of the ship. The parachute fills with air and helps to reduce the speed of the fast-moving spaceship. For people who enjoy the sport of skydiving, a parachute is the most vital part of their outfit!

Terminal Velocity

After jumping from an airplane, a skydiver accelerates just like any other falling object. However, as the sky-diver's downward speed increases, so does the friction between the diver and the air (*air resistance*). By extending his or her arms and legs spread-eagle fashion, the skydiver increases the force of the air on his or her body. When the upward push due to air resistance becomes as large as the skydiver's weight, the diver falls at a constant speed of about 190 kilometers (120 miles) per hour. Any object falling through air will eventually fall at a constant speed. This constant speed, which depends on the weight, shape, and area of the falling body, is called *terminal velocity*.

To increase air resistance still more and to ensure a safe return to earth, the skydiver opens a parachute. The parachute catches still more air, increasing the upward force on the diver's body. This time, the increased force reduces the skydiver's speed until weight and air resistance are again equal. At this much-reduced terminal velocity, the diver falls slowly to the ground.

A Model Parachute

To make a simple parachute of your own, tie the ends of four pieces of thread, each about 25 centimeters (10 inches) long, to the corners of a large handkerchief. Tie the other ends of the threads to a metal washer (see Figure 35). The washer represents the skydiver. Close your hand around the handkerchief, thread, and washer. Then throw them up into the air. What happens? Compare the rates of fall of the parachute and washer with a washer without a parachute.

Another air sport that many enjoy is piloting a long-winged glider back to earth after it has been towed into the sky by an airplane and released. These gliders descend much more slowly than parachutes. You have probably made a model glider—better known as a paper

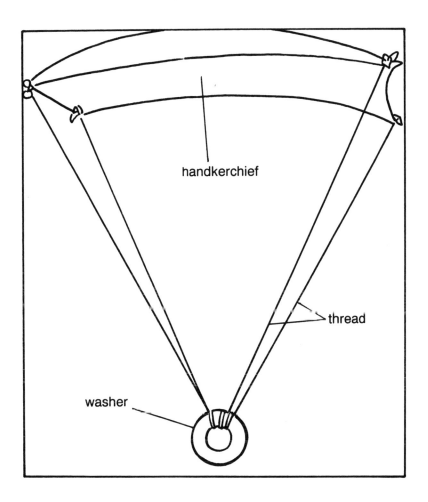

handkerchief

thread

washer

35) A model parachute.

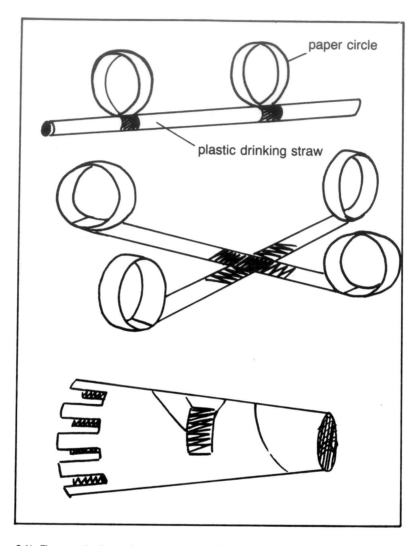

paper circle

plastic drinking straw

36) Three designs for paper models of gliders. How many
more can you design? Which one glides best?

airplane. Design and make a variety of paper airplanes. Three models that you may not have tried are
shown in Figure 36.

The force of gravity on the surface of a planet depends on the amount of matter in the planet and on the planet's radius. On the earth's surface, the force of gravity causes objects to accelerate as they fall. The speed of a falling object increases by 9.8 meters (32 feet) per second every second it falls. On our own moon, objects fall with an acceleration of 1.7 meters (5.6 feet) per second every second.

Things That Go Bump in the Night (or Day)

Things that are moving often bump into one another. This is true of the tiny molecules of air moving at average speeds of 1,800 kilometers (1,100 miles) per hour, as well as people and cars moving at much slower speeds. It is less true of the objects that move through space, such as meteoroids, comets, planets, moons, and stars. But the craters on the moon reveal that celestial objects moving through space do bump into each other from time to time.

Bumping molecules and bumping people or cars are very different. Collisions between molecules and atoms are usually *elastic*. Collisions between automobiles or people who bump into one another are either only *partially elastic* or *inelastic*.

During elastic collisions, no motion energy is lost; the speeds of the colliding objects are very much the same before and after the collision. In an inelastic collision, all the energy of motion is changed to heat. For example, suppose a car bumps into a tree. The car was moving before the collision. After the collision, the car has lost all its motion energy and the tree is still at rest; the collision was inelastic.

4.1   GRAVITY, FALLING, AND COLLISIONS

To do this experiment you will need:
- 30-centimeter (12-inch) grooved ruler
- balls or spheres, such as baseballs, basketballs, tennis balls, lacrosse balls, soccer balls, marbles, ball bearings, etc.
- marble
- rubber ball
- modeling clay
- yardstick

Gravity

From Newton's laws of motion, you know that if an object starts to move, or begins to move faster or slower, a force is acting on the object. Hold a ball at rest several feet above the floor. Release the ball and it begins to move downward. Any object denser than air will fall toward the earth when you release it. *Gravity* is the name we give to the force that makes objects fall. Any two masses are pulled toward one another by the force of gravity. But the force is very small. Two objects, each weighing a ton, placed one foot apart, will attract one another with a force that is about equal to the weight of 5.7 grams (0.2 ounce). Only the earth has enough mass (about a billion trillion tons) to pull on objects with any significant force.

Everything is attracted (pulled) towards the earth. To see that the force of gravity makes an object accelerate toward the earth, try this: Drop a ball from a height of 1 meter (3 feet). At the moment you release the ball, begin counting aloud, "1, 2, 3, 4, 5 . . ." as fast as you can. (It takes about one second to count to five as fast as you can.) You will find that you can count to about four before the ball strikes the floor. If the ball moves at a steady speed after you release it, it should take twice as long to fall 2 meters (6 feet). If it accelerates, it should take less than twice as long to reach the floor from a height of 2 meters (6 feet).

Release the ball from a height of 2 meters (6 feet). At the moment you release the ball, begin counting. How far did you count before the ball struck the floor? What evidence do you have that the ball accelerated as it fell?

Measuring a "Fall"

Galileo, who lived before clocks were invented, measured time with a water clock. He used the amount of water that flowed from a container as a measure of time. Galileo soon realized that the time it took for most objects to fall to the ground was too short to measure accurately with his water clock. To lengthen the times of fall, he used round objects that would "fall" (roll) down an incline (a hill) rather than letting them fall straight toward the earth.

Try Galileo's method yourself. Let a marble roll down a grooved ruler, as shown in Figure 37. One end of the ruler should be raised about an inch. You can measure time as you did before by counting as fast as you can. How far can you count while the ball rolls 15 centimeters (6 inches) down the ruler? How far can you count while the ball rolls 30 centimeters (12 inches) down the ruler? How do you know that the ball accelerates?

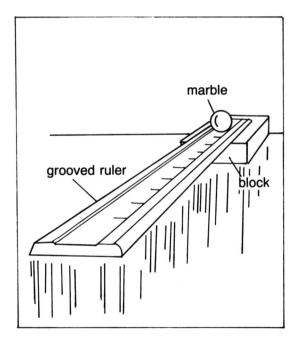

37) Galileo's method of diluting gravity.

Collisions

When a falling object falls and bumps into the earth, the collision might be elastic, inelastic, or partially elastic. Remember, in an elastic collision, no motion energy is lost; the speeds of the colliding objects are very much the same before and after the collision. In an inelastic collision, all the motion energy is lost; it is changed to heat.

Drop a clay ball onto a floor. How do you know that the collision is inelastic? Drop a rubber ball onto a floor. How do you know that the collision is *not* inelastic? If the collision is elastic, the rubber ball's speed after the collision will be as great as it was before the collision. If the rubber ball's speed is the same after the collision as it was before, the ball will rebound to the height from which you dropped it. Design and carry out an experiment to find out whether the rubber ball's collision with the floor was elastic or partially elastic. What do you find?

Drop a number of other spheres such as baseballs, basketballs, tennis balls, lacrosse balls, soccer balls, marbles, ball bearings, and other round, unbreakable objects. Which ones make inelastic collisions with the floor? Which ones collide elastically? For which ones is the collision partially elastic?

4.2   GRAVITY, MASS, AND FALLING

To do this experiment you will need:
- two balls of different mass, such as a baseball and a tennis ball
- dime or small metal washer
- 30-centimeter (12-inch) ruler
- table or counter
- quarter or larger washer

From lifting different objects, you know that the force of gravity depends on the mass of the object. You have to pull harder to lift a 4.5-kilogram (10-pound) bag of potatoes than a 0.45-kilogram (1-pound) loaf of bread. In fact, an object with twice as much mass is pulled twice as hard by the earth's gravity. From Newton's second law of motion, you know that if the force on a mass doubles, its acceleration doubles too. If the same force acts on twice as much mass, the acceleration of the mass will be half as big. So, what happens when the earth's gravity acts on objects of different mass?

If the mass doubles, the force of gravity doubles. But, according to Newton's second law, when the mass doubles, the acceleration halves. Since 2 x 0.5 = 1, we must conclude that the acceleration of all falling objects should be the same, regardless of their mass (see Figure 38).

To test that idea, drop two objects of different mass from the same height. You might use a baseball and a tennis ball. Hold the balls at the same height above the floor and release them at the same time. Do they reach the floor at about the same time? What do you conclude about their accelerations?

Testing the Acceleration of Falling Objects

Because it is difficult to release two balls at exactly the same time, you might try another experiment. In this experiment, you can be sure that both objects begin their fall at the same time. Place a ruler near the edge of a table or counter, as shown in Figure 39. Place a dime

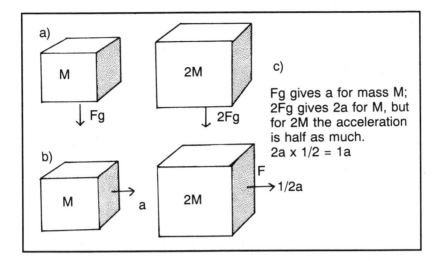

a)

M

$\downarrow$ Fg

2M

$\downarrow$ 2Fg

b)

M

a

2M

c)

Fg gives a for mass M; 2Fg gives 2a for M, but for 2M the acceleration is half as much.

2a x 1/2 = 1a

F

→1/2a

38a) When the mass doubles, the force of gravity doubles too. When the mass triples, the force triples, and so on.

b) Newton's second law of motion tells us that for the same force, doubling the mass will have half the acceleration.

c) If the force doubles and the mass doubles, the acceleration will stay the same because 2 x 0.5 = 1.

on the end of the ruler that extends beyond the table. Place a quarter on the edge of the table near the other end of the ruler. Use the index finger of one hand to hold the ruler against the tabletop, as shown in the drawing. Strike the ruler sharply with your other hand at the point shown by the arrow. Because of its inertia, the dime will not move with the ruler. But without the ruler beneath it, it will fall to the floor. The heavier quarter will be pushed off the table at the same time. It will also fall to the floor as it travels horizontally.

After you hit the ruler, listen carefully. Do the coins hit the floor at the same time? What can you conclude?

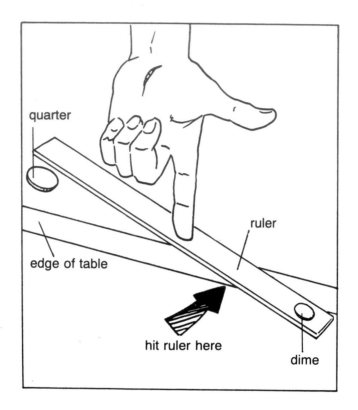

quarter

edge of table

ruler

hit ruler here

dime

39) Are the downward accelerations of two falling coins the same even if their masses are different?

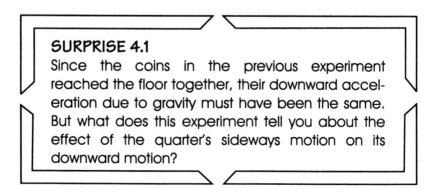

SURPRISE 4.1
Since the coins in the previous experiment reached the floor together, their downward acceleration due to gravity must have been the same. But what does this experiment tell you about the effect of the quarter's sideways motion on its downward motion?

4.3   NEARLY ELASTIC COLLISIONS

To do this experiment you will need:

- toy with swinging steel spheres (see Figure 40)
- 11-millimeter (7/16-inch) or larger steel spheres (ball bearings, which can be found in many hardware or automotive stores or large glass marbles (agates))
- grooved ruler, container with grooves, or two boards or yardsticks
- small marble

If you have a toy with swinging steel spheres that looks like the one in Figure 40, you can use it to make nearly elastic collisions. If not, you can use 10-millimeters (7/16-inch) or larger steel spheres or large glass marbles (agates) on a grooved ruler or container or in a slot between two boards or yardsticks taped to a counter, as described on pages 95-96. There will be more friction if you roll the steel balls (or marbles). The swinging spheres move through air so there is less friction and their collisions are more nearly elastic.

If you have the toy with swinging steel spheres, pull one steel ball away from the others and release it. After the one moving steel sphere collides with the other steel balls at rest, how many spheres move away on the other side? How does the speed of the sphere on the other side compare with the one that you pulled back and released? What happens next?

Repeat the experiment, but this time pull two balls back and release them. What is different about the collision? See if you can predict how many balls will swing away after the collision when you pull back three balls and release them. Try it! Were you right?

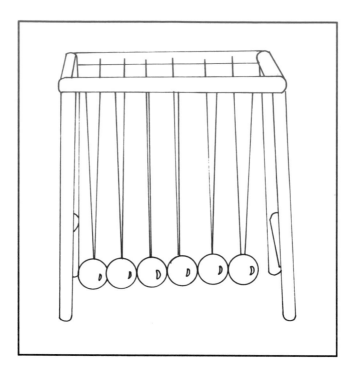

40) A toy with swinging steel spheres.

Predict how many balls will swing away after the collision if you release four and then five balls. Were your predictions correct?

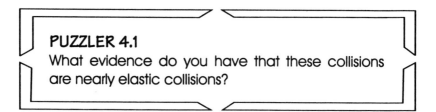

PUZZLER 4.1
What evidence do you have that these collisions are nearly elastic collisions?

Creating a Rolling-sphere Toy

If you do not have the toy with swinging spheres, you can make a rolling-sphere toy using identical steel spheres (ball bearings) or marbles (agates). The ball bearings or marbles can be rolled along a grooved ruler, grooved container, or along a straight pathway made by taping two yardsticks or small, straight boards side by side, as shown in Figure 41. The space between the sticks should be slightly wider than the diameter of the balls.

Using the ball bearings or marbles, you can do the

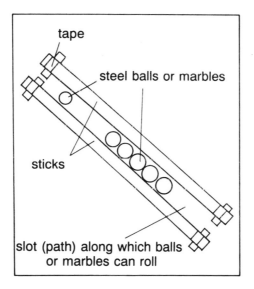

41) Top view of a homemade rolling-sphere toy.

experiment described above for the swinging spheres. Simply place about six steel balls or marbles on the level grooved ruler or container or in the slot between the sticks. Then take one ball and roll it into the others.

Roll two balls together into the others and so on. What do you find? How does friction affect the experiment?

Identifying Collisions

Place just one ball on the groove or in the pathway. Roll a second identical ball into the one at rest, as shown in Figure 42a. Would you describe the collision as elastic, inelastic, or partially elastic? Why?

Repeat the experiment, but this time place your finger firmly on top of the ball at rest (see Figure 42b). Then roll the other ball into it. What evidence do you have that this collision is inelastic or nearly so?

Try to predict the outcome of each of the series of experiments shown in Figure 42c. For which ones were you able to predict the results? Which ones were inelastic collisions? Were any of the collisions elastic? Were any partially elastic?

Roll a small marble into a much larger marble or steel sphere, as shown in Figure 42d. What happens to each ball after the collision? Now turn the experiment around. Roll the heavier ball into the lighter one. What happens this time? Were these collisions elastic, inelastic, or partially elastic?

PUZZLER 4.2
Based on what you saw when the large ball and the small ball collided, why is it safer to be in a large car or truck than in a small car during a collision?

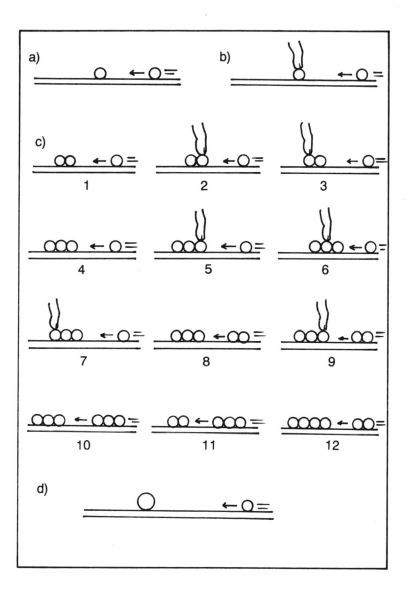

42) Experiments with spheres on the rolling-sphere toy.

4.4   SOFTENING BUMPS ON HIGHWAYS

Highway engineers, car designers, legislators, and inventors are always looking for ways to make automobile travel safer. Lanes are made wider; vehicles traveling in opposite directions are often separated by wide concrete, shrub, or metal medians to prevent head-on collisions and to absorb light from oncoming headlights; reflectors are placed along lane markers to make them more visible at night; dangerous intersections are well lighted and preceded by warning signs; and so on. Many states have passed laws that require automobile passengers to wear seat belts, and many automobiles now have inflatable air bags to reduce the forces on passengers during a collision.

Seat Belts

Seat belts are designed to hold passengers firmly against the seat of the vehicle in which they are riding and to prevent them from being thrown into the windshield or out through a window if a collision occurs. Statistics show that a person is much more likely to be injured or killed if thrown from a vehicle than if he or she is held within it. You can see the effect of seat belts in a collision by doing a simple experiment.

4.5   A SEAT BELT EXPERIMENT

To do this experiment you will need:

- small doll
- smooth, level surface such as a driveway, sidewalk, or concrete floor
- strong rubber bands
- large toy truck or car
- smooth wide board
- two concrete blocks

The purpose of this experiment is to see how a seat belt can reduce the danger involved in an automobile collision. You can use a small doll to represent a passenger in a car. Strong rubber bands will serve as a seat belt to fasten the doll to a large toy truck or car, as shown in Figure 43.

Make a ramp or "hill" from a wide board. Rest one end of the board on a concrete block to form the incline. Let the toy truck roll down the hill and accelerate

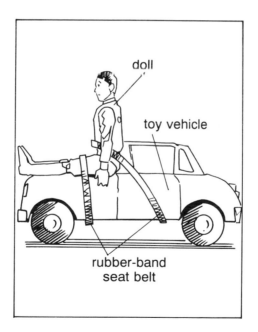

doll

toy vehicle

rubber-band
seat belt

43) A rubber band seat belt holds the doll to the vehicle.

onto a smooth, level surface such as a driveway, side-walk, or concrete floor.

Place a concrete block near the end of the ramp. Leave enough space so that the toy truck or car can roll a short distance on the level surface before it hits the block. Then let the toy vehicle and its passenger, with seat belt in place, roll down the incline and collide with the heavy block of concrete. What happens to the truck or car? Is the passenger thrown from the vehicle when it crashes?

Now, repeat the experiment without the seat belt. What happens to the passenger during the collision this time? Based on your experiments, do you think seat belts save lives?

PUZZLER 4.3
How can Newton's laws of motion help to explain the value of seat belts?

4.6   A SAFER CRASH?
ONLY AN EXPERIMENT CAN TELL

To do this experiment you will need:
- smooth, wide board
- smooth, level surface such as a driveway, sidewalk, or concrete floor
- two concrete blocks
- large toy truck or car
- pencil
- about a dozen tin cans

At many highway intersections, you may have seen large plastic barrels filled with sand. The barrels are often placed in front of concrete barriers. If a car goes out of control at the intersection, it will collide with the barrels of sand instead of the concrete barrier. This experiment will help you to find out whether such barrels make collisions less dangerous.

Use a smooth, wide board and concrete block to make a ramp as you did in the previous experiment. Place the toy truck or car at the top of the ramp and let it roll down the hill and across a smooth, level surface. How far does the vehicle roll before it stops? Indicate its stopping place with a pencil. Repeat the experiment several times to be sure the distance the vehicle rolls is about the same each time.

Crashing into Concrete

Place a concrete block near the end of the ramp. Leave enough space so that the toy truck or car can roll a short distance on the level surface before it hits the block. Let a large toy truck or car roll down the ramp and collide with the block. Watch the toy vehicle closely when it hits the block. What happens to the vehicle during the collision?

Repeat the experiment, but this time watch the concrete block. What happens to the heavy block during the collision? What would be likely to happen to a passenger in the vehicle? You can see that during such a collision the concrete is not going to "give." It will be the car that will change its shape.

Crashing Into Tin Cans

Now replace the concrete block with about a dozen tin cans. The cans represent the sand-filled barrels found at some highway intersections. Let the toy truck or car roll down the ramp and collide with the "barrels." Watch the vehicle during the collision. Does it stop as suddenly as it did when it hit the concrete, or does it stop more gradually? How does the distance it rolls compare with the distance it traveled when it rolled freely across the level surface?

Repeat the experiment. This time, keep your eye on the barrels. Do they remain in place the way the concrete did, or do they "give" as the car hits them?

Why would a passenger be more likely to survive a collision between a car and barrels of sand than one in which the car hits a concrete barrier?

4.7   CLAY CARS: A BETTER MODEL

To do this experiment you will need:
- modeling clay
- two concrete blocks
- smooth, wide board
- about a dozen tin cans

A toy vehicle is very light. Unlike a heavy car or truck, it may bounce off a heavy object. A ball of clay is less springy than toy cars. In many ways it is a better model of a real car than is a toy vehicle. It will bend or squash more like a real car when it hits something.

Let a large ball of clay roll down a steep ramp and bump into a concrete block at the base of the ramp. What happens when the clay hits the block? Look at the clay. How has it been changed by the collision? Repeat

the experiment using the tin cans in place of the concrete. Again, examine the clay after the collision. How
was this collision different from the previous one?

PUZZLER 4.4
How can Newton's laws of motion be used to explain why barrels of sand provide a safer barrier
than concrete?

Answers To Puzzlers and Surprises

Puzzler 1.1

Because the sheet is smooth, there is very little friction between the cup and the plastic. When you pull the sheet quickly, the small force of friction has very little time to act on the cup—the sheet is gone before the force has moved the cup very far. If you pull slowly, the frictional force acts on the cup long enough to make it move a significant distance.

Surprise 1.1

The coin will remain at rest unless acted upon by a force. Because the card is so smooth, it exerts very little force on the coin when it moves beneath it. Therefore, the coin remains where it was and falls into the cup as the card moves out from under it.

Surprise 1.2

The liquid in the uncooked egg has inertia. You stopped the egg, but the liquid inside the shell continued to move. When you release the egg, the moving liquid inside the shell pushes against the shell and puts the egg back into motion.

Surprise 1.3

The petroleum jelly reduces the friction between your hand and the door knob. Lack of friction may prevent you from turning the knob.

Puzzler 1.2

When a constant force acts on the ball, its speed increases by the same amount each second; it accelerates uniformly. If the force doubles while the amount of matter remains the same, the acceleration doubles. If the amount of matter (mass) doubles and the force is constant, the acceleration will be half as much.

Puzzler 1.3

To make the spaceship accelerate forward, we could start the rocket engines and fire gases backward (opposite to the direction the spaceship is moving). According to the third law of motion, the gases would exert an equal force in the forward direction on the ship, causing it to accelerate forward. To make the ship slow down or decelerate, we could use rocket engines that fire their exhaust fuel forward. The gases would exert an equal force backward on the ship, causing it to decelerate (slow down). The space shuttle uses such methods to maneuver in space. It is launched into orbit by giant rocket engines that accelerate it to speeds of nearly 29,000 kilometers (18,000 miles) per hour. After the fuel in these large engines has burned, the engines are released and fall back to earth. The shuttle and its smaller onboard engines continue into an orbit about the earth.

Puzzler 2.1

Normally, you push against the earth when you walk and Newton's third law of motion applies—the earth pushes against you. But the earth is much more massive than you. Its acceleration backward is practically nothing compared to your acceleration forward. When you try to take a step by pushing backward against the board, which rests on rollers, there is very little friction between the rollers and the smooth surface. The board, like the earth, pushes forward on you with an equal force. But, unlike the earth, the board has much less mass than you do. Consequently, it accelerates backward much faster than you accelerate forward.

Puzzler 2.2

A horse has to accelerate from rest (speed = 0) to reach its maximum speed (64 kilometers or 40 miles per hour). During this time, the horse's average speed might be 32 kilometers (20 miles) per hour. Consequently, a horse's average speed over the race is less than its fastest speed.

Puzzler 2.3

In Experiment 2.4, you learned that to convert feet per second to miles per hour you multiply by 0.68. Thus, if you find that a worm moves 3 feet in 1 minute, its speed in feet per second would be:

$$\frac{3.0 \text{ feet}}{60 \text{ seconds}} \quad = \quad 0.05 \text{ feet per second}$$

Its speed in miles per hour would be: 0.05 feet per second x 0.68 miles per hour = 0.034 miles per hour.

Puzzler 2.4

The swimmer had a speed of:

$$\frac{328 \text{ feet}}{48.63 \text{ seconds}} = 6.75 \text{ feet per second}$$

It's speed in miles per hour would be: 6.75 feet per second x 0.68 miles per hour = 4.6 miles per hour.

This is about the same as the speed at which most fish swim, but considerably less than faster fish such as tuna and barracudas.

Puzzler 3.1

The wheel and pedals would turn in opposite directions. In Figure 23, notice that if gear 1 turns in the direction that the hands of a clock turn, gear 2 will turn in the opposite direction. Because the gears on a bike are connected by a chain, the wheel, pedals, and gears to which they are connected turn in the same direction.

Puzzler 3.2

Most of the space within the boat is filled with air. Air is much less dense than water. The overall weight of the boat—metal and air—is less than the weight of an equal volume of water. Think of a metal soup can. When the can is filled with soup, it sinks because it weighs more than an equal volume of water. When it is filled with air, it floats because the can and air together are less dense than water.

Surprise 3.1

While the cup is falling, the water is weightless. It accelerates downward at the same rate as the cup. The water exerts no force against the bottom or sides of the cup.

Surprise 4.1

Since both coins strike the floor at the same time, their downward accelerations must be the same. However, the quarter moves horizontally as well as downward. The quarter's downward acceleration is not affected by its horizontal motion. Once the coins left the rulers, the only force acting on them was gravity, which pulled them straight downward; there was no horizontal force. Consequently, Newton's first law of motion tells us that the quarter's horizontal speed must have been constant once it left the ruler.

Puzzler 4.1

The steel balls continue to swing back and forth for a long time. This indicates that little motion energy is lost during each collision.

Puzzler 4.2

When a small object bumps into a large one, the large object moves away with less speed than the small object had before the collision. The small object stops and, if the collision is somewhat elastic, may bounce backward. If the small object were a car, someone in the car would experience a much bigger acceleration than would someone in the large car or truck. On the other hand, when a large object strikes a small one, the large object loses speed but continues to move in the same direction. The small object actually moves away faster than the large object. Again, if the objects are cars, passengers in the small car experience larger accelerations and are, therefore, more likely to be injured than those in the large car or truck.

Puzzler 4.3

During a collision, a seat belt keeps a passenger fastened to the seat of the vehicle in which he or she is riding. As a result, the passenger decelerates at the same rate as the vehicle. Without the seat belt, the passenger would continue to move in the same direction, at the same speed the vehicle was traveling before the collision—a path that could send him or her through the windshield.

Puzzler 4.4

The force on a vehicle colliding with the less massive, less rigid barriers of sand is less than if it collides with rigid concrete. The smaller force acts over a longer period of time to stop the vehicle than does the larger force in a collision with a rigid concrete barrier. As a result, the vehicle decelerates more slowly. This reduces the damage to the vehicle and the danger to its passengers.

Further Reading

Alexander, R. McNeill. *Exploring Biomechanics: Animals in Motion.* New York: Scientific American, 1992.

Ardley, Neil. *Making Things Move.* New York: Watts, 1984.

_____ . *The Science Book of Motion.* New York: Harcourt Brace, 1992.

Cobb, Vicki. *Why Doesn't the Earth Fall Up and Other Not Such Dumb Questions About Motion.* New York: Lodestar Books, E. P. Dutton, 1988.

Gardner, Robert and David Webster. *Moving Right Along.* Garden City, N.Y.: Doubleday, 1978.

Lafferty, Peter. *Force & Motion.* New York: Dorling Kindersley, 1992.

Kerrod, Robin. *Moving Things.* London: Macdonald, 1987. Morristown, N.J.: Silver Burdett, 1987.

Taylor, Barbara. *Force and Movement.* New York: Watts, 1990.

Walpole, Benda. *Movement.* New York: Warwick, 1987.

Watson, Philip. *Super Motion.* New York: Lothrop, Lee, & Shepard, 1982.

Index

A acceleration, 17–20,
   34, 87, 88, 90–92
action and reaction, 26
air car, 15
airplanes, 71–73
air resistance, 81
antelope, 33
astronaut, 12, 23

B balloon submarine, 29
barracudas, 55
Belmont Stakes, 43
bicycles, 58 63
   brakes, 62–63
   gears, 59–61
birds, 47–48, 50
blowhole, 54
boats, 67–71
bones, 51, 56
brakes, 62–64, 71
   cars, 64–67
   on ice, 67

C cannon bone, 41
cars, 63–67
cheetahs, 33
chicken bones, 51
collisions, 85–103
   elastic, inelastic,
      partially elastic,
      85–86
   nearly elastic,
      93–97

concertina motion,
   44–45
crawling, 46, 47

D deceleration, 34, 69
dolphins, 54, 55

F femur, 41
fibula, 41
fins, 54
first law of motion,
   10, 12–14
fish, 52–56, 57
flight, 47–48, 49–51
force and acceleration,
   17–21
friction, 7, 63, 81
frictionless air car, 15

G gaits (horse), 42
Galilei, Galileo, 8
gears, 59–61
gliders, 81, 82, 84
gravity, 8, 65, 73, 75, 86

H highway safety, 98,
   100–103
horses, 41, 42
human motion, 34–40

I inertia, law of, 9

J jet engines, 72–73
jet-powered cup, 31–32

K Kentucky Derby, 43
knee cap, 38

M motion
    animals, 33–57
    concertina, 44–45
    constant force,
      21–23
    first law of, 10, 12–14
    human, 34–40
    in space, 7–31
    second law of,
      17–21, 90
    serpentine, 44–45
    sidewinding,
      44–45
    swimming, 52–56
    third law of, 23–32,
      52, 53, 67, 72
muscles, 37–38

N Newton, Isaac, 7

O orbital motion, 75–76,
    78, 79

P paper airplanes, 84
parachutes, 81, 82
    gliders, 81
propellers, 68, 70, 71

R retro-rockets, 76
rockets, 29–30, 73–74
roller coaster, 79

rudders, 69
running, 35

S seat belts, 98–100
second law of motion,
    17–21, 90
serpentine motion,
    44–45
sidewinding motion,
    44–45
skydiving, 81
snakes, 44–46
spaceship, 8, 12
space shuttle, 73–76
speed, 39
    fish, 55
    horses, 43
    humans, 39–40
    mammals, 54, 55
squid, 73
submarine (balloon), 29
swim bladder, 52

T tablecloth trick, 11
tendons, 34, 37–38
terminal velocity, 81–82
third law of motion, 23–
    32, 52, 53, 67, 72
tibia, 41
tuna, 55
two-legged motion, 34

U ulna, 37

W walking, 34, 35, 39–40
weightlessness, 76, 80
whales, 54, 55